SUBSTANCE USE DISORDERS

Assessment and Treatment

SUBSTANCE USE DISORDERS

Assessment
and Treatment

Charles E. Dodgen, Ph.D.
Saint Barnabas Medical Center
Livingston, New Jersey

W. Michael Shea, Ph.D.
Center for Evaluation & Counseling
Newton, New Jersey

ACADEMIC PRESS
A Harcourt Science and Technology Company

San Diego   San Francisco   New York   Boston   London   Sydney   Tokyo

Cover photo credit: Photos © 2000 Photodisc, Inc. and © 2000 Corbis Images.

This book is printed on acid-free paper. ∞

Academic Press
A Harcourt Science and Technology Company
525 B Street, Suite 1900, San Diego, California 92101-4495, U.S.A.
http://www.academicpress.com

Academic Press
Harcourt Place, 32 Jamestown Road, London NW1 7BY, UK
http://www.hbuk.co.uk/ap/

Library of Congress Catalog Card Number: 99-68567

International Standard Book Number: 0-12-219160-9

PRINTED IN THE UNITED STATES OF AMERICA
00 01 02 03 04 05 SB 9 8 7 6 5 4 3 2 1

To our children
Danielle and Christopher (C.E.D.)
Caitlin and Douglas (W.M.S.)

TABLE OF CONTENTS

4 Course/Natural History of Psychoactive Substance Use Disorders

5 Prevention, Early Intervention, and Harm Reduction

6 Screening and Assessment of Psychoactive Substance Use

7 Diagnosis and Comorbidity

8 Treatment I: Models and Approaches

9 Treatment II: Planning, Implementing, and Managing Treatment and the Course of Recovery

10 Issues in Specific Populations

11 Legal and Ethical Issues

PREFACE

The epidemic magnitude of substance abuse in the United States is well documented and of concern to professionals and laymen alike. In recognition of this already serious and still growing problem, and of the need for psychologists to be competent to work with psychoactive substance use disorders, the American Psychological Association (APA) College of Professional Psychology recently developed a national certification procedure. The certification procedure was developed to ensure that psychologists are sufficiently knowledgeable to assess and treat substance abusers, as well as to provide consumers with some means to identify those therapists experienced in this area of clinical work.

While writing this, we realized that the information had applications much broader than for psychologists preparing for the specialty exam. Other professionals seeking certification in their respective fields (psychiatrists specializing in addiction medicine, social workers, substance abuse counselors, etc.) are required to master the same information. Furthermore, due to the high prevalence of psychoactive substance use disorders in the general population (higher still for those individuals seeking mental health services) contact with matters of substance use and abuse can hardly be avoided. All clinicians should be familiar with the manifestations of substance abuse regardless of whether they intend to treat the condition. Assessment for potential substance abuse can now be considered a standard component of any diagnostic evaluation. The mandate to be competent to at least assess for alcohol or drug abuse (if not to treat) applies to any clinician: psychologists, psychiatrists and other physicians, social workers, nurses, and substance abuse counselors.

Along with our recognition of the broader applications of the information we were assembling came an increase in breadth and depth of material in our attempt to provide thoughtful discussion of current information on all important aspects of substance abuse for any clinician interested in learning about these matters. For this reason, we went beyond the provision of basic facts that may have been sufficient to pass a professional certification examination. We also endeavored to create a resource for individuals to locate information on psychoactive substance use disorders. Therefore, the publication provides liberal references to source materials, including journal articles, books, and recommended chapters.

We have made no attempt to advance new concepts or to revise existing concepts or procedures. Rather, we aspire to accurately represent the existing literature on psychoactive substance use disorders. We expect that, for those interested in using the book for purposes of exam preparation, having this information in a single source, while no guarantee of success on a professional certification examination, should be an aid in the preparation process and a significant time-saver.

PRESENTATION OF THE MATERIAL

A review of the total universe of available information on psychoactive substance use disorders could easily fill volumes, would be well beyond the scope of this publication, and would serve no practical purpose. In view of the staggering amount of published information, we had to decide which information to present. The knowledge domains assessed by the APA certification exam served as a basis for organization and inclusion of material for this publication.

ACKNOWLEDGMENTS

The authors gratefully acknowledge two psychologists, Dr. Lori Kadish and Dr. Diane Niederhoffer Klein, who provided invaluable assistance during the preparation of the original manuscript. Special thanks to Dr. Klein for her expert editing. Additional thanks to our families for their unwavering and enthusiastic support and encouragement.

CLINICAL PHARMACOLOGY AND CLINICAL EPIDEMIOLOGY OF PSYCHOACTIVE SUBSTANCES

Prior to discussing the pharmacological properties of individual substances, this text will present some discussion of general concepts that can be used to facilitate understanding. Regarding epidemiology, this chapter will explore general trends in substance use prior to presenting information specific to each substance.

DEFINITIONS AND GENERAL CONCEPTS OF PHARMACOLOGY

The information on pharmacology, relative to information in other chapters of this publication, is technical and detailed. The basic principles of pharmacology comprise a store of knowledge best presented in traditional, textbook style.

Pharmacology is "the study of the effects of chemical substances on living systems" (Blum, 1984, p. 10). Due to the obvious risks, most information in pharmacology is obtained from animal studies (Blum, 1984). Several problems arise with the use of animal models:

1. Some difficulties are not predictable across species. Doses of a drug may have no effect when tested on nonhumans but may have a significant effect on humans.

2. In animal studies, thousands of subjects are employed. In actual drug usage, millions of people are involved so that seemingly insignificant problems may be very significant with larger scale use.

3. Some cognitive, behavioral and social effects of substances cannot be predicted from nonhumans.

Tolerance is a condition in which "repeated doses of the same amount of drug become diminishingly effective and progressively larger doses are required to secure a desired effect" (Blum, 1984, p. 6). Tolerance develops to different degrees across classes of substances (American Psychiatric Association, 1994). For example, opioid and amphetamine users may develop substantial tolerance; alcohol and nicotine users may develop tolerance to a lesser degree. Tolerance to marijuana has been demonstrated in animals, not clearly in humans; tolerance to hallucinogens has not been established for humans.

Withdrawal is a "maladaptive behavioral change, with physiological and cognitive concomitants, that occurs when blood or tissue concentrations of a substance decline in an individual who had maintained prolonged heavy use of a substance" (APA, 1994, p. 178). As with tolerance, the intensity of symptoms varies by drug class. Withdrawal symptoms are most apparent for opioids, alcohol, and other central nervous system (CNS) depressants (i.e., sedative-hypnotics and anxiolytics). Less obvious withdrawal symptoms are observed for CNS stimulants. For many drugs (e.g., opioids, CNS depressants, amphetamines, nicotine) the abstinence reaction is the opposite of the drug effect (Blum, 1984). For example, amphetamines increase energy and elevate mood; the abstinence syndrome is associated with low energy and depression. Protracted abstinence refers to abstinence/withdrawal symptoms that last for as long as several months. Withdrawal symptoms are listed in DSM IV (APA, 1994) and are reviewed in Chapter 6.

An intoxication syndrome is "a reversible, substance-specific syndrome due to the recent ingestion of a substance", and the syndrome "is characterized by clinically maladaptive behavior or psychological changes" (APA, 1994, p. 183).

A toxic reaction, also known as an overdose, "is a reaction to a drug that indicates the subject is under the influence of the noxious, undesirable effects of that particular drug" (Blum, 1984, p. 690). Opioids and CNS depressants most frequently result in toxic overdoses (Schuckit, 1995).

Half-life refers to the time required for half the amount of a substance to be eliminated from the body (Johanson, 1992). Generally speaking, the longer the half-life, the longer the duration of action in the body. Substances with a shorter half-life tend to deliver a more intense "high" and, therefore, have an elevated abuse potential.

Cross-dependence is "the potential of one drug to take the place of another, and to suppress the symptoms of physical dependence of the substituted drug" (Blum, 1984, p. 6). Typically, drugs within the same class can be used interchangeably. For example, one opioid can be substituted for another; often, alcohol will be used by abusers of other CNS depressants (e.g., barbiturates, benzodiazepines) to suppress withdrawal symptoms when the other substances are not available. Cross-dependence is also relevant in the discussion of medical detoxification. The general rule of detoxification is to substitute a drug with a longer half-life for one in the same class that has a shorter half-life (Blum, 1984). For example, methadone is used for detoxification of heroin; both drugs are in the same class (opioid) and methadone has a longer half-life than heroin. Methadone does not produce the intense euphoria that heroin does and it stays in the system longer than heroin, softening the withdrawal symptoms.

Cross-tolerance refers to "the development of tolerance to other drugs in the same class" (Blum, 1984, p. 7). For example, if a person has a tolerance for cocaine, that person will also have a tolerance for another CNS stimulant such as amphetamine.

For a drug to have an effect on an individual, it must enter the body. Routes of administration significantly affect the rate at which a drug enters the bloodstream and reaches the brain. In general, the quicker a drug reaches the brain, the more intense the response. Also, in general, the faster a drug enters the bloodstream, the shorter its half-life because once in the bloodstream and circulated to the liver, the substance is broken down and eliminated. Due to the effects on the intensity of response and half-life, route of administration relates significantly to abuse potential.

The routes of administration are presented here in order from slowest to fastest entry into the bloodstream (Blum, 1984; Johanson, 1992):

1. Oral.
2. Mucosa. The mucous membranes under the tongue, in the nose, and in the rectum are richly vascularized, allowing for faster entry into the bloodstream than the oral method.
3. Inhalation. This is a very effective means of introducing drugs into the bloodstream; drugs move efficiently from the lungs into the bloodstream and easily pass into the brain. Only the intravenous injection of drugs results in a more rapid entry into the bloodstream. One special consequence of this method is that, due to entrance into the circulatory system via the lungs, some portion of the drug is distributed before the liver has a chance to metabolize it (i.e., chemically break the drug down); there is no "first-pass" effect in the liver. The first-pass effect refers to "the degradation and loss of a drug on its requisite passage through the liver to the general circulation" (Johanson, 1992, p. 37). Drugs entering the circulatory system via all other methods are more quickly metabolized by the liver.
4. Injection. Drugs can be injected in three ways: below the skin (subcutaneous-SC), into the muscle (intramuscular-IM), or into the bloodstream directly (intravenous-IV). The IV method is the most direct and fastest way to introduce a substance into the bloodstream.

In addition to the route of administration, many other factors partially determine the intensity of a drug effect (Blum, 1984):

1. Dose. Generally speaking, the larger the amount of drug, the greater the effect.

2. Tolerance. The greater the tolerance, the larger the amount needed to produce a given effect.
3. General personality structure of the user.
4. Emotional state of the user at the time the drug is taken.
5. Social setting at the time the drug is taken. Marijuana and LSD effects appear particularly vulnerable to setting. Opioid effects are least modified by setting as the users are often semiconscious.
6. Pharmacological nature of the drug.
7. Body weight. Greater body weight requires relatively more of a drug to produce a given effect.
8. Age. Children and older persons are often more sensitive to drug effects.
9. Medical status. Liver dysfunction, for example, will greatly alter the metabolism of drugs in the body.
10. Drug interactions. The effect of a given drug may be altered by the presence of other substances in the body.
11. Gender. Women are generally more sensitive to the effects of substances than are men.

Once the drug is introduced into the body and enters the bloodstream, it is quickly distributed throughout the body; blood circulates completely every minute (Johanson, 1992). Two events occur once the blood is circulated: the drug begins to act on the target site (e.g., the brain), and the body begins to metabolize and eliminate the drug. The liver is the primary organ responsible for metabolism of drugs; drugs and drug metabolites (products of metabolism) are eliminated mainly through the kidneys and, to a lesser degree, the feces (Blum, 1984; Johanson, 1992).

Drugs in the bloodstream do not have completely free access to the brain. Although the brain is highly vascularized, the blood-brain barrier protects the brain from foreign substances; the pores in the capillary walls of the CNS are relatively small and restrict movement of drug molecules into the brain. Drugs that are fat-soluble enter the brain more easily than water-soluble drugs.

Understanding how drugs affect the brain and its functioning requires some knowledge of basic physiology (for a more comprehensive review, see Johanson, 1992). The cells in the brain are called neurons. Neurons essentially consist of three sections: dendrite, cell body, and axon. The dendrite is the part of the neuron that receives information from adjacent neurons. The cell body appears to integrate the input from the dendrites. The axon transmits information to adjacent neurons. Neurons function very simply: they either "fire" (i.e., transmit excitation) or they do not. Information received from other neurons either excites or inhibits the cell's firing. A single neuron can receive information from thousands of other neurons. Once excited (i.e., it has enough stimulation to reach a threshold), an electrical impulse travels from the dendrite, across the cell body, to the cell axon. The neurons are not directly connected to one another; there is a minute gap between axon and adjacent dendrites of other cells. The excitation is communicated to the dendrites of subsequent neurons biochemically—that is, the information travels within neurons electrically and between neurons biochemically. The gap between axon and dendrite is called the synapse. In any given connection, the axon is referred to as presynaptic and the dendrite as postsynaptic.

The neurotransmitters are biochemicals manufactured and stored in the presynaptic axon. Six different types of neurotransmitters have been identified:

1. acetylcholine
2. dopamine
3. endogenous opioid neuropeptides
4. gamma-aminobutyric acid (GABA)
5. norepinephrine
6. serotonin

Excitation in the presynaptic cell results in the release of the neurotransmitters into the synapse which diffuse across the synapse, and affect the postsynaptic dendrite. The neurotransmitters bind to sites on the surface of the dendrite called receptors. Receptors are specific—that is, only certain neurotransmitters can bind with a given receptor. After a neurotransmitter is released, two reactions normally occur: the neurotransmitter binds to receptor cells of the postsynaptic dendrite; then the neurotransmitter is deactivated either by re-uptake by the presynaptic cell or by metabolism.

It is important to understand the neurotransmitters and the functioning at the synapse because modification of this process underlies the actions of drugs. There are several ways for drugs to alter functioning at the cellular level: (a) drugs may affect biochemical transmission by disrupting a cell's production, storage, or release of neurotransmitters; (b) drugs may interfere with neurotransmitter interaction with receptors, or (c) drugs may impede the deactivation of the neurotransmitter (Johanson, 1992). Drugs alter neurotransmission, affect CNS functioning, and create behavioral change (Dykstra, 1992). For example, cocaine prolongs neuronal activity by blocking re-uptake of neurotransmitters, producing excessive stimulation. Some drugs have an effect on the brain by binding with receptor sites, due to their structural similarity to neurotransmitters, and alter the cell's functioning. There are two important concepts related to drug–receptor interaction: affinity and intrinsic activity (Johanson, 1992). Affinity refers to "the ability of a drug molecule to bind to a receptor" (p. 39). Intrinsic activity refers to "the ability of the molecule to produce an effect once it is bound" (p. 39). Drugs that bind and produce an effect are called agonists. Drugs that bind and have a partial effect are called partial agonists. Drugs that bind and have no effect on the postsynaptic cell are called antagonists.

Drugs can be classified in many ways. One way that they can be classified is by pharmacological effects on the CNS. Blum (1984) described such a classificatory system:

1. Narcotics. Opioids such as opium, heroin, codeine, morphine, and methadone are classified as narcotics.

2. CNS depressants. Alcohol, barbiturates, benzodiazepines, and solvent inhalants are considered CNS depressants.
3. CNS stimulants. CNS stimulants include amphetamine, methamphetamine, cocaine, caffeine, and methylphenidate (Ritalin).
4. Psychotomimetics (also known as psychedelics or hallucinogens). Cannabinoids, LSD, mescaline, and psilocybin are classified as psychotomimetics.

Another commonly encountered classification system is that by the U.S. government. This system is not of great clinical value. Drugs are classified with respect to two axes: abuse potential and medical usefulness (Lawson & Cooperrider, 1988; Schuckit, 1995). There are five levels, referred to as schedules. From level one to five, abuse potential theoretically decreases and medical usefulness increases.

1. Schedule I. Schedule I drugs are substances with high abuse potential and low medical usefulness (e.g., heroin, marijuana, hallucinogenic drugs).
2. Schedule II. Schedule II drugs include opium, morphine, codeine, and amphetamines.
3. Schedule III. Aspirin with codeine and PCP are classified as Schedule III drugs.
4. Schedule IV. Phenobarbital and diazepam (Valium) are examples of Schedule IV drugs.
5. Schedule V. Codeine mixtures are classified as Schedule V drugs. These drugs have high medical usefulness and low abuse potential.

PHARMACOLOGY OF INDIVIDUAL DRUGS

In the following discussion of the effects of individual drugs, the amount of drug that will result in behavioral, cognitive, and bodily changes cannot be specified due to the large number of factors involved. Therefore, it is difficult to state a specific relationship between amount of drug consumed and particular physiological changes, degree of intoxication, and toxicity. The general rule is that greater amounts will result in more significant alteration in functioning at all levels. The presentation and discussion of the specific effects of each drug on the user found throughout the pharmacology section, including acute psychological and bodily effects, toxic reactions, and symptoms of chronic use, derive principally from several sources (APA 1994; Blum, 1984; Gold, 1991).

Central Nervous System Stimulants

Major drugs of abuse classified as central nervous system (CNS) stimulants include cocaine, amphetamines, and caffeine (Blum, 1984).

Cocaine

Cocaine is obtained from the leaves of the coca plant found mostly in Colombia and other South American countries (Blum, 1984; Gold, 1986). Cocaine is usually sold in its salt form (cocaine HCL) and in this form is a white, water-soluble powder. Cocaine is usually "cut" (adulterated) with sugars and other substances to increase volume and weight and is of 30 to 50% purity on the street. Cocaine functions as a local anesthetic and served as surgical anesthesia prior to the 1900s.

Cocaine users have various methods of ingesting this substance. The most common route of administration is intranasal (IN) (i.e., "snorting") (Blum, 1984; Gold, 1991). When snorted, the user may experience 20 to 40 min of stimulation depending on the amount consumed. When taken orally, cocaine is broken down by the digestive system and is not effective. Cocaine can also be inhaled. Cocaine powder cannot be smoked; "crack" cocaine is specially prepared to be smoked. Or cocaine can be smoked in "freebase" form, but the user must prepare the drug by mixing it with a volatile substance such as ether. When smoked, the cocaine reaches the brain very quickly (within 7 s) and produces an almost instantaneous, intense rush. Cocaine can also be taken intravenously to produce an immediate rush. However, because cocaine has vasoconstrictive properties, blood vessels collapse, impeding long-term IV use. Smoking and IV methods result in the fastest absorption, most intense rush, but also the shortest duration of action (and therefore, a more intense dysphoria when the drug is being removed from the body, fueling the compulsive desire for more drug). Cocaine is sometimes used in tandem with heroin as a "speedball," but is more frequently used with alcohol.

After absorbed into the bloodstream cocaine is metabolized by the liver (Blum, 1984; Gold, 1991) and may be excreted unchanged or as a metabolite.

Cocaine is a CNS stimulant with properties similar to those of amphetamine (Blum, 1984; Gold, 1991; Ondrusek, 1988). The duration of action is shorter for cocaine than amphetamine. Cocaine appears to produce its effects on the brain by altering the operation of epinephrine, norepinephrine, and dopamine; re-uptake of these neurotransmitters is blocked leaving excess amounts to restimulate receptors (Blum, 1984).

Effects of Cocaine Use

1. Acute psychological effects
   a. Elevation of mood (euphoria)
   b. Increased self-confidence and self-esteem
   c. Improved mental performance
   d. Immunity to fatigue
   e. Increased energy and productivity
   f. Improved sexual performance
   At higher doses:
   g. Stereotyped and repetitive behaviors
   h. Impaired judgment

2. Acute bodily effects
   a. Chills
   b. Nausea or vomiting
   c. Chest pains
   d. Cardiac arrhythmias
   e. Increased heart rate
   f. Elevated blood pressure
   g. Dilated pupils
   h. Constriction of peripheral blood vessels
   i. Increased body temperature
   j. Increased respiration
   k. Decreased appetite
   l. Increased metabolic rate

The positive effects of cocaine, like all other drugs, correspond to ascending levels of the drug in the bloodstream. As the level peaks and diminishes, irritability, dysphoria, and craving for more of the drug are experienced (the "crash") (Blum, 1984, Gold, 1991).

3. Toxic reaction
   a. Restlessness
   b. Agitation
   c. Intense anxiety
   d. Tremors
   e. Muscular twitching
   In severe cases:
   f. Delirium and hallucinations
   g. Death from depression of medullary centers, cardiac or respiratory arrest, seizures, or acute hypertensive crisis
4. Symptoms of chronic use
   a. Disruption of eating (with weight loss)
   b. Disturbance of sleeping habits
   c. Impairment of concentration and memory
   d. Irritability and mood swings
   e. Social isolation
   f. Paranoia
   g. Loss of interest in pleasurable activities
   h. Impairment in family, work and financial functioning
   i. Diminished libido
   j. Depression

Disturbances in mood and behavior can last as long as 10 or more weeks following abstinence from cocaine (Blum, 1984; Gold, 1986; Ondrusek, 1988).

Medical risks of cocaine abuse are partially related to the typical route of administration (Blum, 1984; Gold, 1986). Chronic snorting can result in nasal dripping, chronic rhinitis, upper respiratory infections, and septal necrosis (i.e., cell death of the nasal septum). Smoking cocaine can lead to disturbances of lung structure and function, and upper gastrointestinal (GI) and throat problems. Intravenous use of cocaine can result in endocarditis (inflammation of heart tissue), angina, heart attacks, septicimia (blood poisoning), hepatitis, and AIDS.

Amphetamines

Amphetamines include amphetamine (Benzedrine), methamphetamine (Methedrine), and methlyphenidate (Ritalin). They are synthesized in laboratories and have been used medically for weight control, narcolepsy, performance enhancement, and attention deficit hyperactivity disorder (ADHD) (Blum, 1984; Gold, 1986).

Amphetamines are taken orally (in pill form), snorted, or injected intravenously. Methamphetamine (also known as "speed" and "ice") is a particularly potent form of amphetamine. Amphetamines chemically resemble the neurotransmitters epinephrine and norepinephrine, thus accounting for their stimulating effect on the central nervous system. When taken orally, the effects are experienced within 60 to 90 min (much sooner if taken IV) and may last 2 to 4 hr, depending on the amount consumed (Blum, 1984).

Amphetamines are metabolized by the liver and excreted unchanged or as metabolites via the kidneys (Blum, 1984).

Effects of Amphetamine Use

1. Acute psychological effects
   a. Elevated mood (euphoria)
   b. Inflated feelings about self (e.g., sense of invulnerability or of superior capabilities)
   c. Paranoia
   d. Hyperactivity (e.g., increases in motor and speech activity)
   e. Stereotyped and repetitive behavior
2. Acute bodily effects
   a. Perspiration or chills
   b. Nausea or vomiting
   c. Diminished appetite
   d. Reduced need for sleep
   e. Mild analgesia
   f. Increased heart rate
   g. Elevated blood pressure
   h. Dilation of pupils

As with cocaine use, when blood levels of amphetamine peak and diminish, severe dysphoria and fatigue are experienced.

3. Toxic reaction
   a. Chest pain
   b. Unconsciousness or, if awake, inability to move or talk

In severe cases:

   c. Psychotic reaction that mimics paranoid schizophrenia

4. Symptoms of chronic use
   a. Cardiac damage
   b. Liver damage
   c. Malnutrition and weight loss
   d. Paranoid states
   e. Amphetamine (paranoid) psychosis
   f. Depression
   g. If IV administration is employed, the individual is at risk for all needle-related illnesses.

Caffeine

Caffeine, a naturally occurring CNS stimulant, is found in everyday beverages including coffee and tea, as an additive in soft drinks, and in pill form (e.g., NO-Doz) (Blum, 1984). The drug is typically taken orally. Caffeine is used to increase energy and alertness. The mechanism used by the drug to stimulate the central nervous system is not known. The half-life of caffeine is approximately 2.0 to 4.5 hr.

Caffeine is easily absorbed through the digestive system, metabolized by the liver, and excreted via the kidneys (Blum, 1984).

Effects of Caffeine Use

1. Acute psychological effects
   a. Mood elevation
   b. Reduction of fatigue
   c. Enhanced performance of motor tasks

In large doses:

   d. Restlessness
   e. Muscle twitching
   f. Nervousness
   g. Excitement
   h. Psychomotor agitation

2. Acute bodily effects
   a. Diuresis
   b. Gastrointestinal disturbance
   c. Flushed face
   d. Insomnia

3. Toxic reaction
   a. Tachycardia
   b. Headache
   c. Hypotension
   d. Convulsions
   e. Respiratory failure

4. Symptoms of chronic use
   a. Anxiety
   b. Agitation
   c. Depression
   d. Hallucinations
   e. Delusions
   f. Elevated risk of cardiovascular disease
   g. Elevated risk of pancreatic cancer

There are no abuse, dependence, or withdrawal syndromes listed in DSM IV for caffeine (APA, 1994).

Nicotine

Nicotine is classified by itself, despite the fact that it has some properties similar to CNS stimulants. At higher doses nicotine also has properties of CNS depressants. Nicotine is derived from the leafy green tobacco plant (Blum, 1984). Commonly used tobacco products are cigarettes, cigars, snuff, chewing tobacco, and pipe tobacco. The various products are consumed in different ways (Blum, 1984): cigarette smoke is inhaled, pipe and cigar smoke are not. Snuff is either sniffed into the nose, placed in the cheek, or placed between the lower lip and gum. Chewing tobacco is placed in the cheek and the juice is spit out.

Nicotine is absorbed through the membranes of the mouth, nose, and lungs (Blum, 1984). Once in the bloodstream, it is metabolized by the liver and lungs; nicotine is excreted in the milk of lactating women who smoke. The half-life of nicotine is 20 to 30 min. Nicotine is extremely toxic—some cigars contain enough nicotine for two lethal doses. Fortunately, however, only very small amounts of nicotine are actually inhaled with the smoke. Nicotine exerts its effects on the body by altering the operation of norepinephrine and acetylcholine.

Effects of Nicotine Use

1. Acute psychological effects
   a. Feeling of relaxation
   b. Feeling of well-being
2. Acute bodily effects
   a. Increased heart rate
   b. Increased blood pressure
   c. Increase in bowel activity
   d. Vasoconstriction of the skin
   e. Suppressed appetite
   f. Increased acid in the stomach
3. Toxic reaction
   a. Nausea
   b. Vomiting

     c. Dizziness

     d. General weakness

In severe cases:

     e. Respiratory paralysis

     f. Tremors

     g. Convulsions

Medical risks of nicotine abuse are well known (Blum, 1984; Gold, 1991). Some of the risks of smoking, in particular, may be due to other substances in tobacco (e.g., carbon monoxide as well as hundreds of other compounds have been isolated in tobacco).

    4. Symptoms of chronic use of cigarettes

     a. Heart disease

     b. Chronic bronchitis

     c. Pulmonary emphysema

     d. Bronchial asthma

     e. Visual problems

     f. Ulcers

     g. Cancer of the lip, tongue, tonsils, larynx, lungs, stomach, intestine, pancreas, and bladder

     h. Cigarette smoking during pregnancy has harmful effects on the fetus.

There is no intoxication syndrome in DSM IV for nicotine (APA, 1994).

Central Nervous System Depressants

The CNS depressants that will be discussed are alcohol, barbiturates, and the benzodiazepines. All CNS depressants produce effects along a continuum (Blum, 1984):

    1. Antianxiety

    2. Sedation

    3. Hypnosis (altered state of consciousness resembling sleep)

    4. Anesthesia (loss of sensation)

    5. Coma

    6. Death

Alcohol

Alcohol is the most widely abused substance in the United States (Blum, 1984; Schuckit, 1995) It is, ironically, not thought of as a drug; the phrase "alcohol and drug abuse" fallaciously suggests that alcohol is in a category by itself. Although alcohol can be inhaled, it is almost always consumed as a beverage. The principal ingredient of all alcoholic beverages is ethyl alcohol (also known as ethanol or alcohol). The percentage of alcohol varies by the product. For example, beer is approximately 4% alcohol, wine 12%, liquors 22% to 50%, and distilled spirits 40% to 50%. Alcohol, a depressant, is sometimes mistakenly thought of as a stimulant; the increased energy that is observed is due to increased blood sugar and decreased inhibition (Blum, 1984).

Alcohol is rapidly absorbed into the bloodstream from the stomach, small intestine, and colon. Several factors affect the rate of absorption of alcohol into the bloodstream (Blum, 1984):

1. The presence of food in the stomach. If food is present absorption is slower.
2. The time it takes to consume the beverage. The more rapidly consumed, the faster the absorption.
3. Emptying time of the stomach. The faster it empties, the more rapid the absorption.
4. Body weight. The higher the body weight, the less rapid the absorption.
5. Characteristics of the beverage. The higher the alcohol content, the more rapid the rise in blood alcohol content.

Alcohol is eliminated from the body by excretion via breath, urine, and sweat, and by metabolism in the liver (via the enzyme alcohol dehydrogenase). The effects from a single drink last approximately 1 hr (unless additional drinks are consumed) (Blum, 1984; Schuckit, 1995).

Effects of Alcohol Use

1. Acute psychological effects
   a. Relaxation
   b. Mild sedation
   c. Disinhibition
At higher levels:
   d. Incoordination
   e. Slurred speech
   f. Nystagmus
   g. Impairment in attention and memory
   h. Confusion
   i. Impaired judgment
   j. Disorientation
At very high (toxic) levels:
   k. Stupor
   l. Coma
   m. Respiratory depression
   n. Death

The effects of alcohol on a given individual may be modified by age, weight, sex, and tolerance (Schuckit, 1995). Alcohol exhibits cross-tolerance with other CNS depressants and with opioids; alcohol and heroin are frequently used together.

2. Toxic reaction
   a. Alcohol by itself is not highly toxic, but when combined with other drugs its toxicity increases (e.g., barbiturates).

3. Symptoms of chronic alcohol use
   a. Damage to the liver
   b. Cardiac muscle damage
   c. Damage to circulatory, gastrointestinal, and genitourinary systems
   d. Brain damage. Wernicke-Korsakoff Syndrome describes the extreme end of the spectrum of cognitive impairment resulting from chronic alcohol abuse.
   e. Teratogenic effects. Fetal alcohol syndrome (FAS) is characterized by adverse CNS effects (microcephaly, developmental delay, mental retardation, and abnormal neuronal integration), growth retardation, and characteristic facial distortion (Blum, 1984; Gold, 1991).
   f. Accidental injuries due to impairment in cognition, visual-motor functioning, and judgment (Gold, 1991).

The dose-related effects of alcohol are well documented (Blum, 1984; Schuckit, 1995) and presented as follows:

1. Blood alcohol content of 0.0 to 19 (mg/100ml blood). Mild sedation and relaxation may be observed.
2. Blood alcohol content of 20/99 (mg/100ml blood). Impairment of motor coordination and diminished reaction time may be observed.
3. Blood alcohol content of 100/199 (mg/100ml blood). More severely impaired coordination, impairment of judgment, and decreased mental activity may be observed.
4. Blood alcohol content of 200/299 (mg/100ml blood). Slurred speech, marked incoordination, impaired judgment, and labile mood may be observed.
5. Blood alcohol content of 300/399 (mg/100ml blood). Anesthesia, memory impairment, labile mood, and loss of consciousness may be observed.
6. Blood alcohol content of 400 (mg/100ml blood) and higher. Respiratory failure, coma, or death may occur.

Barbiturates

Barbiturates are synthetic compounds prepared in pill form (Blum, 1984). This class of CNS depressants can be dissolved and injected. However, the most common route of administration is oral. A barbiturate is any derivative of barbituric acid. More than 2500 compounds have been synthesized, although only about a dozen are commonly used. Barbiturates have been used medically to reduce restlessness and tension and to induce sleep. They have also been used to treat epilepsy. Barbiturates (and other CNS depressants including alcohol) appear to produce their effects by altering the operation of the neurotransmitter GABA. They are usually classified by duration of action as follows (Blum, 1984):

1. Ultra short-acting barbiturates (duration of action from 15 min to 3 hr). These drugs are used as IV anesthetics and include drugs such as sodium methohexital (Brevital), sodium thianylal (Surital), and sodium thiopental (Pentothal).

Shorter-acting barbiturates produce the most intense intoxication and have the highest abuse potential.

2. Short- to intermediate-acting barbiturates (duration of action from 3 to 12 hr). These drugs are used as sedative-hypnotic agents and include such drugs as amobarbital (Amytal), sodium butabarbital (Butisal), sodium pentobarbital (Nembutal), and secobarbital (Seconal).

3. Long-acting barbiturates (duration of action from 12 to 24 hr). These drugs are used as sedative-hypnotic agents and include phenobarbital (Luminal).

Barbiturates are well absorbed from the stomach. Short-acting barbiturates are absorbed more rapidly than long-acting ones (Blum, 1984). Alcohol enhances absorption, thereby increasing medical risk. Barbiturates are metabolized by the liver and excreted via the kidneys.

Effects of Barbiturate Use

1. Acute pscyhological effects
   a. Relaxation
   b. Reduced tension
   c. Improved sleep

At higher levels:
   d. Cognitive impairment such as diminished concentration and problems with attention and memory
   e. Inappropriate sexual or aggressive behavior
   f. Mood lability
   g. Impaired motor behavior (e.g., slurred speech, incoordination)
   h. Impaired judgment
   i. Irritability
2. Toxic reaction
   a. Coma
   b. General shock syndrome (i.e., weak rapid pulse, decreased blood pressure, cold, sweaty skin)
   c. Death due to respiratory arrest, cardiovascular collapse or kidney failure

Barbiturates have often been used as a means of suicide.

Benzodiazepines

Benzodiazepines are CNS depressants and include such drugs as chlordiazepoxide (Librium), diazepam (Valium), chlorazepate (Tranxene), chlorazepam (Klonopin), alprazolam (Xanax), and lorazepam (Ativan). They are similar in properties to the barbiturates; however, they are much safer in terms of risk of overdose/toxicity. The benzodiazepines are used medically for treatment of anxiety conditions.

Cannabinoids

Cannabinoids come from the Indian hemp, a tall weedy herb that can be grown in any region with hot summers (Blum, 1984; Gold, 1986, 1991; McCaig & Lawson,

1988). Drugs such as marijuana, hashish, and hash oil are derived from the hemp plant. The active ingredient in these drugs is tetrahydracannabis (THC). Marijuana is approximately 1 to 10% THC; hashish is approximately 15% THC; and hash oil is approximately 60% THC. Therapeutic uses of marijuana include the treatment of glaucoma and control of nausea in cancer chemotherapy.

Marijuana and hash products are usually smoked and are well absorbed into the lungs (Blum, 1984; Gold, 1991). Effects are noticeable within 1 to 5 min, with peak effects observed in 30 to 60 min. Cannabinoids are also cooked in foods (e.g., brownies, cookies) and ingested. When ingested, the effects are diminished.

After absorption into the bloodstream, THC is metabolized by the liver and excreted via the kidneys (Blum, 1984; Gold, 1991).

At low levels, the effects of cannabinoids are similar to CNS depressants such as alcohol (Blum, 1984). At higher doses, hallucinogenic properties are experienced; thus a biphasic response to cannabinoids is observed.

Effects of Cannabinoid Use

1. Acute psychological effects
   a. Elevated mood (euphoria)
   b. Perceptual disturbance (e.g., temporal disintegration—confusion of past, present, and future)
   c. Impairment of motor functioning
   d. Cognitive impairment (e.g., disturbance of short-term memory and concentration)
   e. Depersonalization
   f. Anxiety (especially for inexperienced users)
   g. Paranoia
   h. Impairment of judgment
   i. Short-term psychotic reaction (with hallucinations) has been observed in those who are predisposed.
2. Acute bodily effects
   a. Increased appetite
   b. Dry mouth
   c. Tachycardia
3. Toxic reaction
   a. Nausea and vomiting. No lethal dose has been established for humans.
4. Symptoms of chronic use of cannabinoids
   a. Amotivational syndrome characterized by fatigue and lethargy, poor planning, drug preoccupation, loss of interest in activity, and social deterioration
   b. Medical problems similar to those affecting cigarette smokers in terms of vulnerability to infections and cancers
   c. Infertility

    d. Diminished immune system functioning

    e. Elevated risk of accidental injury and death

There is no withdrawal syndrome listed in DSM IV for cannabis (APA, 1994).

Opioids

Opiates include opium and drugs made from opium: heroin, codeine, and morphine (Blum, 1984). Opioids are substances, natural or synthetic, with morphine-like properties and include the above drugs, and prescription narcotics (e.g., Demerol). Opium is obtained from the opium poppy. Federal law classifies the coca leaf and its derivatives (e.g., cocaine) as narcotic; however, these coca-derived drugs are stimulants and scientists do not consider them narcotic (Blum, 1984). Opioids are used medically for acute, short-term pain relief and to reduce suffering in later stages of terminal illnesses. They are also used for sedation, antitussive action, and gastrointestinal distress. The manufacture and distribution of medicinal opioids are stringently controlled by the federal government.

Effects of Opioid Use

1. Acute psychological effects

    a. Strong sense of euphoria and well-being

    b. Near-stuporous state ("the nod") characterized by drowsiness, slurred speech, impairment in attention, detachment from the environment, respiratory depression, and pupillary constriction

2. Acute bodily effects

    a. Sweating

    b. Nausea and vomiting

3. Toxic reaction

    a. Pinpoint-size pupils

    b. Slow respiration

    c. Death

4. Symptoms of chronic opioid use

    a. Risk of overdose

    b. Malnutrition

    c. Diminished immune system functioning, and vulnerability to infection

    d. Intravenous users are susceptible to multiple illnesses, which may result from dirty needle use.

    e. Because opioids mask pain, potentially serious medical and dental conditions may be neglected.

The duration of effects for most opioids is 3 to 6 hr.

    Narcotic drugs can be classified in four categories (Blum, 1984):

1. Natural opium derivatives. Morphine and codeine are examples of natural opium derivatives.

Psilocybin and Psilocin

Psilocybin and psilocin are derived from mushrooms (Blum, 1984; Gold, 1991) and taken orally. The effects are very similar to LSD except that the duration of action is much briefer.

PCP

PCP is a synthetic drug found in powder form (placed on tobacco and smoked—"angel dust"—or snorted) or taken orally as tablets and capsules (Blum, 1984). PCP was initially investigated as an anesthetic agent; side effects of agitation and delirium were very problematic.

Effects of PCP Use

1. Acute psychological effects
   a. Elevation of mood (euphoria)
   b. Severe cognitive impairment (e.g., confusion, impulsiveness, and impaired judgment)
   c. Behavioral disturbance (e.g., assaultiveness, belligerence, restlessness, and agitation).
   At higher doses:
   d. Symptoms of paranoid schizophrenia

The quality of the "high," which lasts approximately 4 to 6 hr, is strongly influenced by personality and environment.

2. Acute bodily effects
   a. Tachycardia
   b. Nystagmus
   c. Pupillary constriction
   d. Hypertension
   e. Numbness
   f. Loss of coordination (ataxia)
   g. Difficulty speaking (dysarthria)
3. Toxic reaction
   a. Convulsions
   b. Coma
   c. Death
4. Chronic use of PCP
   a. Recurrent psychotic reactions (with hallucinations and delusions)
   b. Chronic depression and anxiety
   c. Memory impairment
   d. Confusional states
   e. Disorientation
   f. Elevated risk of accidental injury

There is no withdrawal syndrome listed in DSM IV for hallucinogens (APA, 1994).

Solvent and Aerosol Inhalants

Substances in this class include gasoline, toluene, amyl nitrate, acetone, ether, and nitrous oxide (Blum, 1984; Young & Lawson, 1988). These compounds are contained in products such as cleaning solutions, lighter fluids, paint thinners, household glues, spray deodorants, spot removers, and nail polish remover. All of these compounds have a similar effect on the CNS: they depress CNS functioning (similar to alcohol intoxication). Cross-tolerance is seen with CNS depressants. Semiliquid compounds (e.g., glue) are inhaled from paper or plastic bags. Liquids (e.g., gasoline) are put onto cloth and put in a paper bag and inhaled. Aerosols are sprayed into a bag or balloon and inhaled.

All inhalants are rapidly absorbed in the lungs and have a rapid onset of action (Blum, 1984). Adolescents are the heaviest users of inhalants for several reasons: the inhalants are accessible and easy intoxicants for adolescents to obtain, they are very cheap, and the effects are of short duration (allowing for many "highs") (Young & Lawson, 1988).

Effects of Inhalant Use

1. Acute psychological effects
   a. Euphoria
   b. Behavioral disturbance (e.g., excitability, belligerence, and assaultiveness)
   c. Apathy
   d. Impaired judgment
2. Acute bodily effects
   a. Dizziness
   b. Nystagmus
   c. Incoordination
   d. Slurred speech
   e. Unsteady gait
   f. Lethargy
   g. Depressed reflexes
   h. Psychomotor retardation
   i. Tremor
   j. Generalized muscle weakness
   k. Blurred vision or diplopia (double vision)
3. Toxic reaction
   a. Stupor or coma
   b. Death may result from arrhythmia or suffocation

There is no withdrawal syndrome listed in DSM IV for inhalants (APA, 1994).

Steroids

Anabolic steroid abuse is engaged in typically by male athletes in an attempt to enhance size, strength, and athletic performance (Banks, 1992). Primary abusers are competitive athletes: power lifters, body builders, and professional football players. Anabolic steroids are derivatives of the hormone testosterone. Steroids can be injected or taken orally in pill form. Side effects of steroid use in men are disturbed sexual/reproductive functioning including sterility, diminished sperm count, diminished libido, and impotence; breast and prostate gland enlargement are also observed (Banks, 1992). Women also experience sexual/reproductive difficulties including menstrual irregularity, sterility, enlargement of the clitoris, decreased breast size, and diminished libido; other problems are observed such as lowered voice, increased bone mass, and male pattern baldness.

Medical consequences of chronic steroid abuse include the following (Banks, 1992):

1. Acne
2. Liver damage
3. Cardiovascular problems (e.g., strokes, hypertension, and heart disease)
4. Allergic reactions
5. Weakness and rupture of ligaments and tendons
6. Chronic fatigue
7. Belligerence ("'roid rage")

CLINICAL EPIDEMIOLOGY OF PSYCHOACTIVE SUBSTANCES

Epidemiology is "the study of the incidence, distribution, prevalence and control of disease in the population" (Bukstein, 1995, p. 33). Measurement of the epidemiology of psychoactive substance use and abuse is primarily conducted with adolescents. There are three sources frequently referred to in order to track trends of substance use and abuse (discussed in Bukstein, 1995; Kaminer, 1994):

1. The National High School Senior Survey (NSS) (also known as the Monitoring the Future Survey), which is a National Institute of Drug Abuse (NIDA) sponsored annual assessment conducted since 1975. In 1991, 15,500 seniors from 136 U.S. high schools were surveyed and in 1991 national samples of 8th and 10th graders were included in the study. The NSS assesses different levels of substance use including (a) lifetime prevalence of substance use (i.e., percent of students who ever used any substances), (b) 30-day prevalence of substance use (i.e., percent of students who used a given substance in the previous 30 days), and (c) prevalence of daily use (i.e., percent who used a given substance daily in the previous 30 days). The NSS also measures attitudes such as perception of harmful effects of drugs, disapproval of drug use, and perceived availability of drugs. A limitation of the NSS is that it only assesses those present at school for the survey, excluding dropouts who are at very high risk for substance use and abuse. The trends of substance use discussed in the next section for each substance are adapted from the senior surveys unless otherwise specified. Because the substances of abuse are illicit, it is assumed that there is some underreporting of use (Bukstein, 1995;

Kaminer, 1994), although the data are generally considered reliable and valid (Oetting & Beauvais, 1990). The prevalence statistics are provided below to illustrate trends of substance use which provide the reader with some gauge of normative use; the numbers are not static and are not meant to be slavishly committed to memory. Every year new prevalence statistics are generated which reflect usually minor adjustments in patterns of use.

2. The National Household Survey on Drug Abuse is a general population survey (conducted by the Department of Health and Human Services). This survey includes household members at and above the age of 12 and has been administered every 2 to 3 years since 1971. Limitations include the exclusion of residents of institutions (prisons, hospitals, etc.) and survey administration at home where an adolescent may be more inclined to deny or underreport substance use (Bukstein, 1995).

3. The Drug Abuse Warning Network (DAWN) is a report of emergency room episodes for substance use-related problems and fatalities and is considered to be a monitor of health consequences of substance abuse trends (Oetting & Beauvais, 1990).

General Trends

Substance-related problems remain the most prevalent mental health issue a clinician will encounter. In general, it has been observed that the age period of the highest prevalence and quantity of abuse is between the midteens and midtwenties (Schuckit, 1995). For most substances, there has been a trend from the late 1980s through the early 1990s toward a decrease in the proportion of individuals using drugs and in the number of individuals having severe problems (Bukstein, 1995). Lifetime prevalence of substance use peaked in the early 1980s, with a 32% decline by 1991. This trend appears to correlate with the attitudes and beliefs of adolescents; perceived harmfulness and disapproval rates of regular substance use have been relatively high from the mid 1980s to the early 1990s. (Kaminer, 1994). However, there have been small increases in use in the early 1990s (through 1993), most significantly for marijuana, LSD, and inhalants. Up until the sixth grade, there appears to be almost no drug use except for cigarettes and alcohol (Kaminer, 1994).

Legal substances for adults (i.e., alcohol, caffeine, nicotine) are considered "gateway drugs" as they are typically the first drugs tried (Bukstein, 1995); the progression usually proceeds to cannabinoids, stimulants/depressants or hallucinogens, then opioids (Schuckit, 1995). Indeed, alcohol, cigarettes, marijuana, and stimulants, respectively, are the four most commonly used drugs by high school seniors (Bukstein, 1995).

Early initiation of use of a given drug predicts later abuse of that and other drugs, especially prior to age 15 (Schuckit, 1995).

In general terms, a higher proportion of male adolescents use substances than female adolescents, especially at higher levels of use (Bukstein, 1995; Kaminer,

1994). There is little difference in the use of stimulants and cigarettes in terms of gender. Native-American adolescents had the highest prevalence rates for cigarettes, alcohol, and most illicit drugs, followed by Caucasian, Hispanic, African American, and Asian adolescents, respectively (Kaminer, 1994). As age increases, the incidence of substance use by African Americans rises, while incidence of use by Caucasians decreases, thus reversing the order of use by these two groups (Kaminer, 1994).

Trends of Specific Substance Use

Alcohol

Over 75% of men and 50% of women in Western countries drink more than an occasional alcoholic beverage (Schuckit, 1995). The highest percentages of drinkers and of alcohol consumption are noted among adolescents and young adults between age 16 to 25. After age 25, there is a decrease with age. Between 25% to 50% of young men experience transient alcohol-related problems such as arguments with friends, missing time from work, and drunk-driving arrests; most never move beyond this level. In their late 20s to early 30s, average drinkers decrease consumption, while problem drinkers maintain or increase their alcohol use.

Over a lifetime, 5 to 10% of adult males in the United States will meet the criteria for alcohol dependence; 17% if the less severe criteria for abuse are included (Schuckit, 1995). Highest rates of alcohol dependence are seen in men aged 30 to 50; rates increase as income, education, and SES decrease. High consumption is noted among Catholics (especially French and Irish). When corrected for SES, most racial or ethnic groups show similar rates of alcohol dependence. Exceptions include low rates of alcohol dependence among Asian Americans and Jewish Americans, and high rates among Native American Indians and Eskimos (Schuckit, 1995).

Lifetime prevalence of alcohol use among high school seniors showed a modest decrease from a peak of 93.2% in 1980 to 87.0% in 1993 (Bukstein, 1995). Monthly prevalence decreased steadily from a peak in 1980 of 72% to 51% in 1993. Daily use also dropped from a peak of 6.9% in 1979 to 2.5% in 1993. Alcohol use is more prevalent and frequent among high school seniors than lower classmen. Alcohol is the substance most frequently used by adolescents, followed by cigarette and marijuana use, respectively.

Other CNS Depressants (Sedative-Hypnotics/Anxiolytics)

CNS depressants are widely prescribed in the United States. Approximately 15% of adults use these drugs during any 1 year; benzodiazepines are the most commonly used by adults (Schuckit, 1995), barbiturates by adolescents (Bukstein, 1995).

CNS depressants are reported in terms of sedatives and tranquilizers. Lifetime prevalence of sedative use peaked at 18.2% in 1975; use declined to a low of 6.1% in 1992 and increased slightly to 6.4% in 1993 (in Bukstein, 1995). Lifetime tranquilizer use exhibited a pattern similar to the sedatives. Tranquilizer use peaked at 18.0% in 1977, decreased to a low of 6.0% in 1992, and increased slightly to 6.4% in 1993.

Monthly sedative use reached a peak in 1975 of 5.4%, declined to a low of 1.0% in 1990, and increased slightly to 1.3% in 1993. Daily use prevalence showed a similar pattern: peak sedative use of 0.3% occurred in 1975; the rate decreased to 0.0% in 1990 and increased slightly to 0.1% in 1993 (Bukstein, 1995).

CNS Stimulants

CNS stimulants are readily available in the United States. Lifetime prevalence of cocaine use showed a significant increase in the 1970s and early 1980s. From a peak of 17.3% in 1985, use declined to a low of 6.1% in 1993 (Bukstein, 1995). Monthly prevalence of cocaine use peaked in 1985 at 6.7% and showed a steady decline to 1.3% in 1993. Prevalence of daily use has also seen a steady decrease from a peak of 0.4% in 1985 to 0.1% in 1993.

All stimulant use (including amphetamines) peaked in 1985 at a lifetime prevalence of 26.2% and decreased steadily to 15.1% in 1993 (Bukstein, 1995). Monthly prevalence of stimulant use peaked in 1980 at 12.1% and declined to 3.7% in 1993. Prevalence of daily use peaked in 1980 at 0.7% and dropped to 0.2% in 1993.

Caffeine

The use of caffeinated beverages is almost universal in Western societies. In the 1970s, 80% of people in the United States had a regular intake of caffeine (Schuckit, 1995). Consumption of colas typically begins in childhood; drinking coffee and tea often starts in the early teens.

Most caffeine consumers drink two or three cups of coffee per day. Consumption appears higher in males and Caucasians. Less educated people and people with fewer religious beliefs also have higher rates of caffeine consumption. Caffeine use tends to increase after age 18 (Schuckit, 1995).

Nicotine (Cigarette Smoking)

The percentage of smokers in most Western countries increased after World War I, reaching a peak in the mid-1960s (Schuckit, 1995). The surgeon general of the United States identified tobacco as a health hazard, helping to produce a significant decline in tobacco use.

Lifetime prevalence of cigarette use among high school seniors was 73.6% in 1975, declining steadily to 61.9% in 1993 (Bukstein, 1995). Monthly prevalence was at 36.7% in 1975, decreasing to 29.4% in 1990, but increasing slightly to 29.9% in 1993. Daily use prevalence steadily decreased from 26.9% in 1975 to 19.0% in 1993.

Marijuana

Although marijuana is used recreationally by people of all backgrounds, the predominant use is among younger people (Schuckit, 1995). The average mari-

juana user is 18 to 27 years old. Among high school seniors, the lifetime prevalence of marijuana use was at 60.3% in 1980, decreasing steadily to 35.3% in 1993
(Bukstein, 1995). Thirty-day prevalence showed a trend that differed from lifetime
prevalence: 33.7% in 1980 declined to 14.0% in 1990 but increased to 15.5% in
1993. Prevalence of daily use of marijuana showed a trend similar to 30-day prevalence: 9.1% in 1980 decreased to a low of 2.2% in 1990 and increased slightly to
2.4% in 1993.

Opioids

Lifetime prevalence of heroin use was at 2.2% in 1975, dropped to 1.1% in
1980, and remained close to this level through 1993 (Bukstein, 1995). Similarly,
30-day prevalence of heroin use was at 0.4% in 1975, dropped to 0.2% in 1980,
and remained at about this level through 1993. Prevalence of daily use of heroin
was at 0.1% in 1975, dipped to 0.0% in 1980, and remained at this level through
1993.

Lifetime prevalence of opioids (other than heroin) peaked in the 1980s; use
was at 10.2% in 1985, with a steady decline to 6.4% in 1993 (Bukstein, 1995).
Monthly prevalence of opioids was at 2.4% in 1980, decreasing steadily to 1.3%
in 1993.

Hallucinogens

Lifetime prevalence of hallucinogen use was at 16.3% in 1975, declining to
9.4% in 1990; an increase to 10.9% was noted in 1993 (Bukstein, 1995). Monthly prevalence of hallucinogen use was at 4.7% in 1975, declining to 2.2% in 1990,
and increasing to 2.7% in 1993. Prevalence of daily use remained at 0.1% from
1975 to 1993. LSD is the most commonly used hallucinogenic drug. Its use was
on the rise in the early 1990s as was the use of other hallucinogens.

Inhalants

Inhalant drugs are typically abused by early adolescents and by others with
limited access to other drugs (Schuckit, 1995). Lifetime prevalence was at 10.3%
in 1976, increasing significantly to 18.1% in 1985, and declining to 17.4% in 1993
(Bukstein, 1995). Monthly prevalence in 1976 was at 0.9%, increasing to 2.7% in
1990, and declining slightly to 2.5% in 1993. Although decreases were noted
in the years from 1990 to 1993, use was well above that of the previous 16 years.
Daily prevalence was at 0.1% in 1980, increasing to 0.3% in 1990, and declining
to 0.1% in 1993.

Steroids

Steroid use was first assessed in 1989 (Bukstein, 1995). Lifetime prevalence
in 1990 was 2.9%, decreasing to 2.0% in 1993. Monthly prevalence was at 1.0%
in 1990, dropping to 0.7% in 1993. Daily use was at 0.2% in 1990 and 0.1% in
1993.

A brief review of the lifetime prevalence statistics reported above through the early 1990s will provide the reader with some idea of normative experimentation by high school seniors. The substances are listed below from most frequently used to least frequently used.

1. Alcohol will be tried at least once by almost 9 out of 10 seniors.
2. Cigarettes will be sampled at least one time by 6 out of 10 seniors.
3. Marijuana use will be attempted at least one time by 4 out of 10 seniors.
4. Inhalants will have been used at least one time by approximately 17 out of 100 seniors.
5. Stimulant use will have been tried by approximately 15 out of 100 seniors.
6. Hallucinogens will be attempted at least one time by approximately 11 out of 100 seniors.
7. Sedative/hypnotics will have been used at least once by approximately 6 out of 100 seniors.
8. Heroin will be tried at least once by approximately 1 out of 100 seniors.

REFERENCES

American Psychiatric Association. (1994). *Diagnostic and statistical manual of mental disorders* (4th ed.). Washington DC: Author.

Banks, R. E. (1992). Steroids. In G. W. Lawson & A. W. Lawson (Eds.), *Adolescent substance abuse: Etiology, treatment, and prevention* (pp. 303–310). Gaithersburg, MD: Aspen Publishers.

Blum, K. (1984). *Handbook of abusable drugs.* New York: Gardner Press.

Bukstein, O. (1995). *Adolescent substance abuse: Assessment, prevention and treatment.* New York: John Wiley & Sons.

Dykstra, L. (1992). Drug action. In J. Grabowski & G. R. VandenBos (Eds.), *Psychopharmacology: Basic mechanisms and applied interventions* (pp. 59–96). Washington DC: American Psychological Association.

Gold, M. S. (1986). *The facts about drugs and alcohol.* New York: Bantam Books.

Gold, M. S. (1991). *The good news about drugs and alcohol: Curing, treating and preventing substance abuse in the new age of biopsychiatry.* New York: Villard Books.

Johanson, C. (1992). Biochemical mechanisms and biological principles of drug action. In J. Grabowski & G. R. VandenBos (Eds.), *Psychopharmacology: Basic mechanisms and applied interventions* (pp. 11–58). Washington DC: American Psychological Association.

Kaminer, Y. (1994). *Adolescent substance abuse: A comprehensive guide to theory and practice.* New York: Plenum Press.

Lawson, G. W., & Cooperrider, C. A. (Eds.). (1988). *Clinical psychopharmacology: A practical reference for nonmedical psychotherapists.* Gaithersburg, MD: Aspen Publishers.

McCaig, J., & Lawson, G. W. (1988). Marijuana. In G. W. Lawson & C. A. Cooperrider (Eds.), *Clinical psychopharmacology: A practical reference for nonmedical psychotherapists* (pp. 243–250). Gaithersburg, MD: Aspen Publishers.

Oetting, E. R., & Beauvais, F. (1990). Adolescent drug use: Findings of national and local surveys. *Journal of Consulting and Clinical Psychology, 58,* 385–394.

Ondrusek, G. (1988). Cocaine. In G. W. Lawson & C. A. Cooperrider (Eds.), *Clinical psychopharmacology: A practical reference for nonmedical psychotherapists* (pp. 201–236). Gaithersburg, MD: Aspen Publishers.

Schuckit, M. A. (1995). *Drug and alcohol abuse: A clinical guide to diagnosis and treatment* (4th ed.). New York: Plenum Medical.

Young, T., & Lawson. G. W. (1988). Central nervous system stimulants. In G. W. Lawson & C. A. Cooperrider (Eds.), *Clinical psychopharmacology: A practical reference for nonmedical psychotherapists* (pp. 137–142). Gaithersburg, MD: Aspen Publishers.

2

ETIOLOGY OF PSYCHOACTIVE SUBSTANCE USE DISORDERS

OVERVIEW

The current literature on the etiology of substance abuse disorders in both adolescents and adults encompasses a range of theories from somewhat simplistic unitary conceptualizations to more inclusive, comprehensive explanatory models. Factors that were once considered elements of competing theories are now more appropriately thought of as complimentary components of a broad model of etiology.

In this chapter, results of genetic research are presented in some detail. However, the major psychological theories (i.e., psychodynamic, behavioral/cognitive-behavioral, and family/systems) are only be briefly summarized. Due to their implications for treatment, the psychological theories are discussed in detail in Chapter 8.

Other etiological factors are also discussed in detail elsewhere in this publication as follows:

1. Cultural/ethnic influences are discussed in Chapters 3, 4, and 10.
2. Peer/social factors are discussed in Chapters 3 and 4.
3. Developmental factors are discussed in Chapters 3 and 4.
4. Biological factors are discussed in Chapter 4.
5. Risk factors are discussed in Chapters 3, 5, and 7.

Following World War II, both the disease model and the psychodynamic theories were considered the most influential explanations for substance abuse disorders (discussed in Bukstein, 1995). Although psychodynamic models of understanding and treatment are currently much less popular than they were previously, the disease model is still considered the most widely accepted model within substance abuse treatment programs. The fundamental premise of this model is that addiction is a disease. The disease is characterized by drug dependence and maladaptive use patterns, as well as the existence of risk for repetition of these patterns throughout the life of the individual (in Bukstein, 1995). Proponents of the disease model point to the facts that a course of illness can be described, etiological factors have been identified, and effective treatments have been developed. The research on the genetic transmission of a predisposition to substance abuse, discussed next, is often cited as hard evidence for the existence of a biologically based disease.

THEORIES OF ETIOLOGY

Genetic Research

Any discussion of genetics must be prefaced with the statement that both genetic and environmental influences affect the ultimate manifestation of a psychoactive substance use disorder. Indeed, very few traits, if any, are determined solely by genetic or environmental factors. The study of the role of genetics in substance abuse aims to determine the relative influence of heredity.

Genetic research has focused almost exclusively on alcohol abuse because it is both legal and prevalent. The possibility of a genetic predisposition to other forms of substance abuse is only recently being investigated.

Studies on the influence of genetics on substance abuse traditionally rely on several methods (Collins & deFiebre, 1990; Crabbe, McSwigan, & Belknap, 1985):

1. Family studies. If traits "run" in families, it is thought that because family members share genes, there may be evidence of a genetic basis for the traits. For example, siblings share approximately 50% of their genetic endowment with each parent and each sibling; nonfamily members obviously share no genes. However, because family members share a common environment, information from family studies, although suggestive of genetic influences, is not conclusive. The study of families is a well-researched area (more than 100 studies have been conducted) that demonstrates that alcohol abuse is familial (discussed in Collins & deFiebre, 1990; and, Crabbe *et al.*, 1985). Approximately 25% of the sons of alcoholics become alcoholics. Also, nearly 33% of alcoholics had at least one parent who abused alcohol. Familial (those with a positive family history) and nonfamilial alcoholic patterns have been described: familial alcoholics have a younger onset, more severe symptoms, and more rapid progression than nonfamilial alcoholics.

2. Study of adoptees. The study of children adopted at an early age helps to untangle genetic and environmental influences on traits. For example, if adopted chil-

dren are more like their biological parents than like their adoptive parents on a given trait, then this result provides support for the impact of genetic influences on the expression of that trait. Multiple studies have found that sons of alcoholics are three to four times more likely to be alcoholic than sons of nonalcoholic biological parents; sons of alcoholics that are adopted by nonalcoholic parents are just as likely as sons raised by alcoholic biological parents to be alcoholic (discussed in Collins & deFiebre, 1990; Crabbe *et al.*, 1985). The observed relationship does not appear as strong for biological mothers and daughters, although a correlation does exist. Adoption studies have identified a genetic predisposition toward two types of alcohol abuse in males: the milieu type and the male limited type. The milieu type is characterized by mild alcohol abuse, minimal criminality, and no history of treatment for alcohol abuse by the biological parents. The male-limited type is characterized by severe alcoholism, high criminality, and history of treatment by the biological father for alcohol abuse. In female adoptees, alcoholism is typically linked to alcoholism in the biological mother and the female pattern resembles the milieu type.

3. Twin studies. Twin studies compare monozygotic (MZ)(identical) and dizygotic (DZ)(fraternal) twins. Monozygotic twins are genetically identical; dizygotic twins share only 50% of their genes like any other sibling pair. In twin studies, researchers compare the similarity (concordance) or dissimilarity of MZ and DZ twins for a given trait. If concordance is higher for MZ than DZ twins, then evidence suggests a genetic influence. MZ twins have been found to have higher concordance for alcoholism than DZ twins in most studies (discussed in Crabbe *et al.*, 1985). It is worth noting, however, that concordance for MZ twins is never 100%, which underscores the significant role of nonbiological, environmental factors.

Human studies have clearly established that risk for alcohol abuse (and probably for other substances) is inherited. Animal studies have been utilized to analyze specific aspects of the genetic predisposition. Substance abuse is a complex behavioral syndrome and is most likely affected by multiple genetic mechanisms. Various aspects of alcohol responses demonstrate a genetic influence (Crabbe *et al.*, 1985):

1. The reinforcing effects of alcohol. Those predisposed to alcohol abuse may find alcohol more reinforcing.
2. Acute sensitivity to the psychotropic effects of alcohol and toxicity. Alcohol abusers have reduced sensitivity to its psychotropic effects and toxic reactions (e.g., nausea).
3. The development of tolerance. Abusers develop tolerance quickly.
4. Withdrawal sensitivity. Abusers may be less sensitive to withdrawal symptoms.

Biological markers have been investigated for early identification of vulnerability to substance abuse suggesting possible physiological, neurological, and psychological bases for this predisposition (discussed in Kaminer, 1994):

1. EEG studies. Sons of alcoholics have demonstrated different brain wave patterns than sons of nonalcoholics.
2. Soft neurological signs. Sons of alcoholics have been found to exhibit greater upper body sway, have inferior memory, language, and psychomotor skills than controls.
3. Cardiac sensitivity. Adults with an alcoholic parent have demonstrated reduced cardiac reactivity to tasks, which suggests decreased attentional processing.
4. Neurotransmitter levels. Some studies posit that a deficit in the brain neurotransmitter, serotonin, is associated with increased risk for alcohol abuse.
5. A diagnosis of ADHD. Attention deficit hyperactivity disorder (ADHD) has been found to be associated with increased risk for alcohol abuse.
6. Personality dimensions (e.g., novelty seeking, harm avoidance). High novelty-seeking and low harm-avoidance personality traits are associated with alcohol abuse.

Psychological Theories

Psychodynamic Theories

The psychodynamic understanding of addiction has evolved along similar lines as psychodynamic theories in general. Early theorists stressed the libidinal aspects of substance abuse such as the fulfillment of a drive for pleasure, hedonism, and the achievement of regressive states. Such conceptualizations of substance abuse were consistent with broader interests in the field in "id" psychology, orality, and the role of drives in determining behavior (Kaufman, 1991; Morgenstern & Leeds, 1993). Contemporary models of substance abuse mirror more recent psychodynamic theories, which emphasize ego development, object relations, and self psychology.

More currently, substance abuse is thought to serve misplaced adaptive and defensive functions. Substance abuse represents an attempt to cope with emotions and the outside world (especially the object world). For example, substance use is seen as serving the function of artificial affect defense (Krystal, 1979). For substance abusers, affects tend to be global, undifferentiated, and preverbal so that the experience of emotions is somatic and overwhelming. The overwhelming bodily experience of emotions leads to drug urges in those unable to analyze, verbalize, and regulate feelings, a condition referred to as alexithymia (Krystal, 1979).

In addition to difficulty with the management of affect, substance abusers may have difficulties with other critical self and ego functions such as maintaining states of well-being and self-esteem, need satisfaction, drive defense, and object relations (Khantzian, 1985). Substances serve a compensatory role, bolstering a beleaguered, inadequate ego, or taming a harsh, punitive superego (Wurmser, 1981).

Current psychodynamic theories of substance abuse share the following beliefs (Morgenstern & Leeds, 1993):

1. Substance abuse is viewed as a symptom of more basic psychopathology.
2. Difficulty in the regulation of affect is seen as a core problem.
3. Disturbed object relations are central to the development of substance abuse.

Behavioral/Cognitive-Behavioral Theories

Behavioral/cognitive-behavioral theories of substance abuse are, by and large, derived from the principles of learning: operant conditioning, classical conditioning, and social learning theory (Rotgers, 1996). The reinforcing aspects of substance abuse (either through generation or enhancement of positive mental states, or diminution or elimination of negative mental states) clearly fit into an operant conditioning paradigm. Classical conditioning principles help to account for the strong association observed between environmental cues and the experience of drug urges. The well-known dictum of AA/NA, "Stay away from people, places, and things," reflects an effort to break the link between environmental cues and substance use.

Key components of social learning theory, as applied to the understanding of substance abuse, include the roles of modeling and cognitive mediation of behavior. Perhaps the best-known risk factor for substance abuse is association with other substance abusers (either in the family or peer group) who model patterns of substance use or abuse. Cognitive factors predisposing an individual to substance abuse include poor problem-solving and coping skills, low sense of self-efficacy (perception of helplessness), and positive expectations of the effects of substances.

Expectancy theorists suggest that the substance abuser becomes aware of the relationship between the use of substances and certain outcomes (discussed in Bukstein, 1995)—that is, an individual learns to anticipate that substance use is related to certain, usually positive, outcomes. The substance abuse behaviors occur when the user anticipates more positive expectations regarding substance abuse than negative ones. These expectancies are thought, at least initially, to be reinforced in the short term. Substance abuse continues as long as an individual's expectancies regarding its use are more positive and greater in number than those associated with the negative expectancies (in Bukstein, 1995).

Stress or tension reduction theory is also largely rooted in cognitive/learning principles. Substance abuse behavior is considered rewarding in that it leads to a reduction in tension including fear, conflict, or frustration (in Bukstein, 1995). The tension reduction theory is based on the reward system of substance use: tension, as it relates to concepts such as fear or anxiety, is reduced via the ingestion of alcohol or other substances. Hence, alcohol and other substances are thought to be utilized in an effort to modulate unpleasant psychological experiences and to reduce tension.

Family Models

There are, essentially, three models of family-based approaches to substance abuse (McCrady & Epstein, 1996):

1. Behavioral. A focus of the behavioral model is on the reinforcing behaviors of family members of the substance abuser. It has been observed that family members often act, unwittingly, in ways that support substance use. For example, a spouse of a substance abuser may prefer (and subtly encourage) the docility of his or her spouse when drinking alcohol to the otherwise irritable and volatile presentation when sober.

2. Family systems. Family systems models focus on the interrelated roles of family members. Changing roles—even the ostensibly negative one of "substance abuser"—is often met with resistance by family members because change requires readjustment of all other family roles. For example, a "caretaker" adolescent may be bumped from his or her role if a substance-abusing parent begins recovery and starts to assume more appropriate family responsibilities.

3. Family disease. The family disease model highlights the fact that not only is the abuser suffering from a disorder, but so also are the other family members. The family members are in need of treatment as well as the abuser; the family disorder partially maintains the substance abuse and without treatment for all, successful recovery for the addict is unlikely.

These family models account for the frequently observed resistance to change, not only in abusers but also in their family members. They also account for factors beyond the individual and speak to the importance of expanding the scope of treatment to include the larger family system.

REFERENCES

Bukstein, O. G. (1995). *Adolescent substance abuse: Assessment, prevention, and treatment.* New York: Wiley & Sons.

Collins, A. C., & deFiebre, C. M. (1990). A review of genetic influences on psychoactive substance use and abuse. In H. B. Milkman & L. I. Sederer (Eds.), *Treatment choices for alcoholism and substance abuse* (pp. 7–24). Massachusetts: Lexington Books.

Crabbe, J. C., McSwigan, J. D., & Belknap, J. K. (1985). The role of genetics in substance abuse. In M. Galizio & S. A. Maisto (Eds.), *Determinants of substance abuse: Biological, psychological, and environmental factors* (pp. 13–64). New York: Plenum Press.

Kaminer, Y. (1994). *Adolescent substance abuse: A comprehensive guide to theory and practice.* New York: Plenum Press.

Kaufman, E. (1991). Critical aspects of the psychodynamics of substance abuse and the evaluation of their application to a psychotherapeutic approach. *The International Journal of the Addictions, 25*(2A), 97–116.

Khantzian, E. J. (1985). The self-medication hypothesis of addictive disorders: Focus on heroin and cocaine dependence. *American Journal of Psychiatry, 142*(11), 1259–1264.

Krystal, H. (1979). Alexithymia and psychotherapy. *American Journal of Psychotherapy, 33,* 17–39.

McCrady, B. S., & Epstein, E. E. (1996). Theoretical bases of family approaches to substance abuse treatment. In F. Rotgers, D. S. Keller, & J. Morgenstern (Eds.), *Treating substance abuse: Theory and technique* (pp. 117–142). New York: Guilford Press.

Morgenstern, J., & Leeds, J. (1993). Contemporary psychoanalytic theories of substance abuse: A disorder in search of a paradigm. *Psychotherapy, 30*(2), 194–206.

Rotgers, F. (1996). Behavioral theory of substance abuse treatment: Bringing science to bear on practice. In F. Rotgers, D. S. Keller, & J. Morgenstern (Eds.), *Treating substance abuse: Theory and technique* (pp. 174–201). New York: Guilford Press.

Wurmser, L. (1981). Psychodynamics of substance abuse. In J. H. Lowinson & P. Ruiz (Eds.), *Substance abuse: Clinical problems and perspectives* (pp. 63–77) Baltimore: Williams & Wilkins.

3

INITIATION, PROGRESSION, AND MAINTENANCE OF PSYCHOACTIVE SUBSTANCE USE DISORDERS

Studies investigating the initiation of use of psychoactive substances and the progression to more serious levels of abuse typically focus on adolescents. Adolescents are usually studied because this is the time when most substance use begins (Swadi, 1992). Substance use can be viewed as part of the developmental process (Bukstein, 1995). That is, substance use is a way for adolescents to experiment with adult behavior and roles, to establish individuality and autonomy, and to join with peers.

STAGE MODELS OF ADOLESCENT SUBSTANCE USE

Stage or sequential models have been constructed by researchers to describe and analyze the initiation and progression of substance use in adolescence (Kandel, 1975, summarized and discussed in Bukstein, 1995; Macdonald & Newton, 1981, summarized and discussed in Muisener, 1994). The Macdonald and Newton (1981) model is called the Adolescent Chemical Use Experience (ACUE) continuum. The ACUE is a four-stage model of adolescent substance use with stages defined in terms of mood swings—that is, a *mood swing* is defined as "the effect of a substance on the internal, subjective state of the person consuming the substance" (Muisener, 1994, p. 4). The four stages of ACUE are described as follows:

1. Experimental stage ("learning the mood swing"). This is the normal adolescent curiosity and experimentation with drugs.
2. Social use ("seeking the mood swing"). This stage is characterized by drug use with peers, occasional excessive use and intoxication, but no chronic problems.
3. Operational use ("preoccupation with the mood swing"). At this stage the criteria for a substance use disorder may be met.
4. Dependent use ("using to feel normal"). At this stage the person will meet the criteria for substance abuse, if not dependence.

The majority of adolescents are at Stages 1 or 2 of the preceding model (Muisener, 1994).

Kandel's (1975) model, widely cited in the literature, is based on longitudinal studies. Kandel's original four-stage model stems from findings that initially adolescents use "gateway drugs"—that is, adolescents experiment with substances that are available and legal for adults: alcohol and tobacco (Bukstein, 1995; Swadi, 1992).

Kandel's (1975) original model is presented as follows:

1. Beer or wine use
2. Hard liquor or cigarette use
3. Marijuana experimentation
4. Other illicit drug use (e.g., opiates)

Further research led to an expansion of the original model (Bukstein, 1995; Swadi, 1992). Alcohol abuse has been added as a stage following marijuana experimentation; also, the nonmedical use of prescription drugs (i.e., stimulants, sedatives, tranquilizers, analgesics) represents another stage between alcohol abuse and use of opiates and other illicit drugs. Kandel's final model, therefore is as follows:

1. Beer or wine use
2. Hard liquor or cigarette use
3. Marijuana experimentation
4. Alcohol abuse
5. Prescription medication use
6. Opiates and other illicit drug use

Almost all adolescents experiment with the gateway drugs with progressively fewer reaching subsequent stages of use (Bukstein, 1995). Adolescents who progress beyond Kandel's first two stages continue to use the gateway drugs, rather than replace them with other drugs (Bukstein, 1995). Whereas the order of progression is generally accepted, the age of initiation and time frame of progression to more serious levels of use and abuse may vary (Bukstein, 1995).

A review of the epidemiological statistics discussed in detail in Chapter 1 generally supports the Kandel model. For example, the percentage of adolescents having ever used alcohol in 1993 was 87%; cigarettes, 61.9%; marijuana, 35.3%; and opioids, 1.3%.

It is well established that almost all adolescents experiment with psychoactive substances, but relatively few progress to the point of substance abuse. Another review of epidemiological statistics from Chapter 1 illustrates this point. For example, in 1993 lifetime prevalence of alcohol use was 87% and alcohol abuse (in terms of daily use) was 2.5%; marijuana lifetime prevalence was 35.3% and abuse was 2.4%. Similarly with heroin, lifetime prevalence was 1.1% and heroin abuse was 0.0%. Note the significant disparity between those who have used at least once (lifetime prevalence) versus those using daily for each of the three substances.

RISK FACTORS

One question of central importance, then, is what factors determine who remains a casual user and who progresses to abuse? In the literature, this question has been addressed through the identification and discussion of risk factors (also discussed in Chapters 5 and 7). The consensus is that many factors contribute to substance use and abuse (Glantz & Pickens, 1992). Substance abuse is the result of the interaction of many factors and no invariant pattern of substance abuse exists (Tarter & Mezzick, 1992).

Bukstein (1995) summarized research across five classes of risk factors for adolescent use and abuse of substances:

1. Peer factors associated with increased risk of substance use or abuse
   a. Peer substance use
   b. Positive peer attitudes toward substance use
   c. Greater attachment to peers (than to parents)
   d. Perception of similarity to peers who use substances
2. Parent/family factors associated with increased risk of substance use or abuse
   a. Parental substance use
   b. Positive parental attitudes about substance use and beliefs about harmlessness of substances
   c. Parental tolerance of adolescent substance use
   d. Lack of attachment between parents and child
   e. Lack of parental involvement with child's life
   f. Lack of appropriate supervision/discipline
   g. Parental antisocial behavior
   h. Family history of psychopathology
   i. Family disruption (e.g., divorce)

3. Individual factors associated with increased risk of substance use or abuse
   a. Early childhood characteristics such as conduct disorder and aggression
   b. Poor academic performance/school failure
   c. Early onset of substance use (especially prior to age 15)
   d. Positive attitudes/beliefs about substance abuse
   e. Risk-taking/sensation-seeking behavior
   f. High tolerance of deviance/nonconformity relative to traditional values
   g. Positive expectancies regarding the effects of substances
   h. External locus of control
   i. Extroversion
   j. Low self-esteem
   k. Poor impulse control
   l. Anxiety/depression
   m. Impaired coping skills
   n. Interpersonal/social difficulties
   o. Traumatic experiences (e.g., childhood physical or sexual abuse)
4. Biological risk factors
   a. Genetically controlled physiological processes and characteristics (e.g., altered sensitivity to alcohol or inherited temperament)
5. Community/social/cultural factors associated with increased risk of substance use or abuse
   a. Low socioeconomic status (SES)
   b. High population density
   c. Low population mobility
   d. Physical deterioration
   e. High crime
   f. Increased unemployment
   g. Deviant norms, which condone abuse of substances
   h. High alienation of the citizens
   i. Availability of substances

Risk Factors for Use versus Abuse

The risk factors identified in the preceding list are for use or abuse; knowledge of these variables still does not totally resolve the question as to who will progress beyond initial use or experimentation. The relative influence of a given factor appears to vary depending on the stage of use (Bukstein, 1995). For example, during the first stage of Kandel's model, environmental influences may be most important, such as prodrug messages from peers, parents, and the media. Progression to the third stage, marijuana use, appears more related to acceptance of beliefs and values favorable to marijuana, involvement with peers who use marijuana, and participation in other deviant behavior (i.e., deviant in terms of lack of adherence to conventional values and standards). Progression to the use of other illicit drugs appears closely related to a poor relationship with parents, psychological distress, heavy marijuana use, exposure to peer and parental drug use models, and involvement in increasingly more deviant behavior.

Stated succinctly, *use* of substances appears more related to curiosity (Morrison & Plant, 1991) and peer/social influences; *abuse* of substances appears more a function of significant psychological distress, poor coping skills, an association of substance use with need satisfaction, and biological predisposition (e.g., substance abusing parent or parental psychopathology) (Cadoret, 1992; Craig, 1995; Glantz & Pickens, 1992; Kaplan & Johnson, 1992). Leeds and Morgenstern (1996) described an illustrative model in which the degree of substance dependence is viewed as a function of different factors. For example, normal use of substances appears to be a function of cultural and social factors. Mild dependence appears more related to psychological processes such as intrapsychic conflict or ego deficits. Moderate to severe levels of dependence appear more a result of biobehavioral processes such as classical and operant conditioning, alteration in the functioning of the brain centers for pleasure and pain, neurotransmitter changes, withdrawal states, and drug cravings.

ADULT MODEL OF SUBSTANCE USE

In contrast to the focus on adolescent development, Vaillant (1996) addressed the initiation and progression of substance use in the context of adult development. Vaillant noted that general patterns of substance abuse are related to age: youth use drugs to produce novelty and excitement, those in midlife use drugs for social purposes, and older adults use drugs to produce quiet and sameness. Vaillant identified four general trends associated with the aging process that affect the use of substances:

1. The ability to tolerate dysphoria increases with age. This lessens the motivation to use drugs in order to change feeling states.
2. Antisocial behavior decreases with age. There is a strong association between antisocial behavior and substance abuse.
3. Emotional maturation occurs allowing for improved relationships. The social motives to use substances are diminished.
4. The effect of drugs is partially dependent on setting, and with advancing age there is less involvement in settings explicitly for partying and using drugs.

REFERENCES

Bukstein, O. (1995). *Adolescent substance abuse: Assessment, prevention and treatment.* New York: John Wiley & Sons.

Cadoret, R. J. (1992). Genetic and environmental factors in initiation of drug use and the transition to abuse. In M. D. Glantz & R. W. Pickens (Eds.), *Vulnerability to drug abuse* (pp. 99–114). Washington, DC: American Psychological Association.

Craig, Robert J. (1995). The role of personality in understanding substance abuse. *Alcoholism Treatment Quarterly, 13*(1), 17–27.

Glantz, M. D., & Pickens, R. W. (Eds.). (1992). *Vulnerability to drug abuse.* Washington, DC: American Psychological Association.

Kandel, D. (1975). Stages in adolescent involvement in drug use. *Science, 190,* 912–914.

Kaplan, H. B., & Johnson, R. J. (1992). Relationships between circumstances surrounding initial illicit drug use and escalation of drug use: Moderating effects of gender and early adolescent experiences. In M. D. Glantz & R. W. Pickens (Eds.), *Vulnerability to drug abuse* (pp. 299–358). Washington, DC: American Psychological Association.

Leeds, J., & Morgenstern, J. (1996). Psychoanalytic theories of substance abuse. In F. Rotgers, D. S. Keller, & J. Morgenstern (Eds.), *Treating substance abuse: Theory and technique.* New York: Guilford Press.

Macdonald, D. I., & Newton, M. (1981). The clinical syndrome of adolescent drug abuse. *Advances in Pediatrics, 28,* 1–25.

Morrison, V., & Plant, M. (1991). Licit and illicit drug initiations and alcohol-related problems amongst illicit drug users in Edinburgh. *Drug and Alcohol Dependence, 27,* 19–27.

Muisener, P. (1994). *Understanding and treating adolescent substance abuse.* Thousand Oaks, CA: Sage Publications.

Swadi, H. (1992). A longitudinal perspective on adolescent substance abuse. *European Child and Adolescent Psychiatry, 1*(3), 156–170.

Tarter, R. E., & Mezzick, A. C. (1992). *Ontogeny of substance abuse: Perspectives and findings.* In M. D. Glantz & R. W. Pickens (Eds.), *Vulnerability to drug abuse* (pp. 149–178). Washington, DC: American Psychological Association.

Vaillant, G. E. (1996). Addictions over the life course: Therapeutic implications. In G. Edwards & C. Dare (Eds.), *Psychotherapy, psychological treatments and the addictions* (pp. 1–18). New York: Cambridge University Press.

4

COURSE/NATURAL HISTORY OF PSYCHOACTIVE SUBSTANCE USE DISORDERS

THE DISEASE MODEL

The discussion of the natural history of psychoactive substance use disorders is based on the premise that a definite condition exists and that its course can be observed and described based on how it is manifested in affected individuals. Jellinek (1960) is credited with one of the first publications utilizing the disease concept of alcoholism. There is currently little doubt or debate as to whether substance abuse is a disease. Webster's dictionary (1955) defines a disease as a destructive process in the body, for which specific causes and characteristic symptoms can be described, and a departure from an established standard of health. The abuse of substances clearly represents a departure from physical and mental health, and unabated abuse ultimately results in destruction of the bodies, minds, and social lives of those individuals (Dodgen, 1994). Causes of substance abuse have been identified (see Chapters 2 and 3), as have characteristic symptoms (see Chapters 6 and 7).

Most people who doubt that substance abuse is a disease are confused by the fact that most of the damage done to an abuser is psycho- (e.g., low self-esteem, emotional dysfunction, mental impairment) social (e.g., damaged relationships, ruined careers, antisocial behavior) rather than physical (although it eventually manifests in physical symptoms) (Dodgen, 1994). The implication in the minds of those who doubt that substance abuse is a disease is that only such conditions as cancer, with identifiable organic manifestations, are "real" diseases. Further confusing people is the fact that the treatment for substance abuse is primarily psychosocial, in the forms of individual and group psychotherapies, and self-help fellowships. What the doubters fail to recognize is that many serious medical conditions have very significant psychosocial and behavioral components contributing to the development of the illness and to the treatment as well—for example, Type 2 diabetes, cardiopathy, and obesity to name a few. No medical intervention will be of much use to a diabetic who does not also cooperate with a comprehensive program of diet, rest, exercise, and stress management, in addition to the use of insulin or oral hypoglycemic agents. Is Type 2 diabetes any less of a disease because its symptoms can be eliminated by behavioral control or because the treatment is largely behavioral and nonmedical?

What substance abuse, other psychiatric conditions, and medical conditions such as obesity have in common is that they are chronic conditions and the effectiveness of the respective treatment programs is largely dependent on the behavior of the patient.

Jellinek (1960), in his classic theory, categorized drinking patterns into four groups, which he thought typified different "species" of alcoholics (discussed in Light, 1985):

1. Alpha alcoholism is characterized by psychological dependence on alcohol.
2. Beta alcoholism is evidenced by long-term daily drinking with eventual medical complications but without psychosocial deterioration.
3. Delta alcoholism is chronic alcoholism with tolerance, withdrawal, and an inability to abstain.
4. Gamma alcoholism is characterized by binge drinking and episodic abuse of alcohol in which periods of uncontrolled drinking are followed by periods of controlled drinking or total abstinence.

Jellinek's (1960) classification system is of interest primarily for historical reasons and is no longer considered valid (Light, 1985). Longitudinal studies with alcoholics demonstrate that patterns of use are highly variable in an individual over time (Vaillant & Milofsky, 1982). A binge drinker (gamma alcoholic) may be a daily drinker (delta alcoholic) at one point in time or abstinent at some other point in time.

Jellinek's (1960) conceptualization of alcoholism as a disease remains an important contribution to the literature. Alcoholism and other forms of substance abuse are considered chronic, progressive, and potentially fatal diseases (Light, 1985). That is, substance abusers cannot be cured, but symptoms may be remitted by avoidance of the substance(s) and care given to related psychosocial factors (Light, 1985). As a progressive illness, a psychoactive substance use disorder is one where the symptoms and consequences become cumulatively worse over time due to continued use of the substance(s) (Light, 1985).

Classic Model of Progression of Alcoholism

Jellinek (1952) (discussed in Light, 1985) also developed the classic model of phasic progression in alcoholism. In this model, the course of alcoholism is divided into four phases of increasing severity:

1. Prealcoholic. The prealcoholic phase is characterized by use of alcohol similar to the nonalcoholic, as a social lubricant. However, the future alcoholic may at this point experience relief from tension and dysphoria not experienced by the nonalcoholic. The prealcoholic phase lasts for variable periods of time through which the drinker moves from drinking to relieve states of dysphoria, to preoccupation with drinking and daily consumption. Drinking becomes a central part of life, but loss of control has not yet occurred, and excesses of drinking may not yet be obvious to self or others.

2. Prodromal. The prodromal phase is characterized by alcoholic blackouts (i.e., memory blackouts associated with an episode of intoxication despite being conscious during this period). Blackouts become a source of intense fear and shame because the individual has no idea what he or she may have done during one of these episodes. Drinking is daily, tolerance and physical dependence are evident, and negative psychosocial consequences become apparent.

3. Crucial. The crucial phase of alcoholism is signaled by loss of control. The individual experiencing loss of control can no longer predict what will happen after a single drink, and negative psychosocial consequences increase in number and severity. The drinker's problem with alcohol is apparent to everyone.

4. Chronic. The chronic phase of alcoholism is characterized by prolonged episodes of intoxication, often lasting for days. Severe medical consequences are evident in this phase, including alcoholic hallucinosis (usually auditory hallucinations), tremors and grand mal seizures during withdrawal, delirium tremens (marked by confusion, profuse sweating, seizures, and elevated temperature), reverse tolerance (a small amount of alcohol can result in intoxication due to liver damage), psychosocial deterioration, Wernicke-Korsakoff syndrome (evidenced by confusion, disorientation, anterograde and retrograde amnesia, and confabulations), and death.

Longitudinal Study of Alcohol Abuse

Jellinek's (1952) observations of phases of alcohol abuse have not held up to longitudinal study (e.g., Vaillant & Milofsky, 1982). Longitudinal studies have demonstrated that there is no single course of alcohol abuse. Rather, over long periods of time the patterns of alcohol consumption and related impairments appear to change. The work of Vaillant and colleagues (Vaillant, Gale, & Milofsky, 1982; Vaillant & Milofsky, 1982) has been seminal in this area.

Vaillant and associates (Vaillant et al., 1982; Vaillant & Milofsky, 1982) reported on a community sample of 456 inner-city men, followed for 33 years (from ages 14–47). Some of the major findings were as follows:

1. Of the 400 men with complete drinking histories, 28% were alcohol abusers.
2. Thirty-two percent of the alcohol abusers exhibited a progressively worsening course (as suggested by Jellinek's model).
3. Fifty-five percent of the abusers were never abstinent; of those who were abstinent, 22% relapsed (i.e., relapses and remissions were common).
4. Some alcohol abusers were able to resume asymptomatic drinking, although these people were the less severely impaired. Those individuals who are less symptomatic are not likely to be seen in a clinician's office.
5. Over time there was significant movement in drinking patterns, demonstrating how cross-sectional studies can be inaccurate and misleading. For example, some people drank abusively at one point in time but drank normally at another point in time.
6. Subjective loss of control was associated with the progressive abuse of alcohol.

Vaillant and Milofsky (1982) concluded that the disease of alcoholism is not defined or best represented by any one symptom or sign but rather by the number and variety of symptoms. The illness for a given individual can vary in terms of presenting symptoms, severity of disability, and treatment response; and the presentation may vary significantly for a given individual depending on the time of assessment. It is important to note that although the preceding discussion focused on alcohol, the course of abuse of other substances may follow the same progression—that is, chronic and, for the more severely symptomatic, progressive (Keller *et al.*, 1992). Because most drugs of abuse are illegal, there may be some slight difference between "pure" alcohol abusers and abusers of other substances in terms of social deviance (Light, 1985).

MODELS OF PROGRESSION OF SUBSTANCE USE

Stage Model of Progression

Shaffer & Robbins (1995) developed a six-stage model to describe the natural history of addiction:

1. Initiation. This stage is represented by the initial experimentation with substances.
2. Positive consequences. This stage is represented by the experience of the direct pleasurable effects of a substance. Psychological benefits (e.g., relief from anxiety or boredom) and social benefits (e.g., peer acceptance) are experienced.
3. Negative consequences. Those that continue to use regularly in pursuit of the positive consequences ultimately experience negative consequences. Negative consequences deter regular use for most users. Those that continue regular use do not link the drug use with the negative consequences.
4. Turning point (initiation of quitting). This is the stage when the abuser be-

gins to recognize that the substance and related behavior are responsible for the negative consequences. This is a time of marked ambivalence.

5. Active quitting. Concrete behavior changes are implemented at this stage, not only in terms of abstinence from the substance of abuse but also in terms of other lifestyle changes.

6. Relapse prevention (change maintenance). This stage is represented by the consolidation of behavior changes and further development of lifestyle changes.

Spontaneous Remission of Substance Abuse

Study of the natural course of any illness is important for at least two reasons: It would be impossible to gauge the effectiveness of treatment without knowing how the untreated illness would naturally progress, and in studying cases of spontaneous remission, natural mechanisms of change and healing may be identified and employed for therapy (Vaillant & Milofsky, 1982; van Kalmthout, 1992).

van Kalmthout (1992) reviewed the literature on spontaneous recovery from substance abuse and identified a number of common elements among those individuals who recovered without treatment:

1. Spontaneous recovery can be triggered by the occurrence of significant life events such as marriage, the start of a new job, and religious conversion on the positive side or personal illness, accident, extraordinary circumstances (e.g., attempted suicide, humiliating events) on the negative side.
2. An existential crisis (also known as "hitting bottom" or "naked lunch") is precipitated by the changes in life circumstances. The individual confronts his/her situation and begins a period of personal reassessment.
3. The existence of economic and social support systems greatly facilitates recovery.

Stages of Change Model

When discussing change and motivation to change, the work of Prochaska and DiClemente is relevant. The Stages of Change Model (Prochaska & DiClemente, 1986) has been applied to the study of addictions. The original model consists of four stages:

1. Precontemplation. At this stage the individual is not thinking about change.
2. Contemplation. This stage occurs when the individual is aware that a problem exists and is thinking about change.
3. Action. This stage occurs when the individual attempts to change.
4. Maintenance. At this stage, successful change is maintained.

Prochaska and DiClemente later added the decision stage to the model, which occurs after the contemplation stage and before the action stage (discussed in Gossop, 1996). An important aspect of the Stages of Change Model is the 10 processes of change (discussed in Sutton, 1996), consisting of the following elements:

1. Consciousness raising. Increasing information about self and problem
2. Self-liberation. Belief in one's own ability to change
3. Dramatic relief. Experiencing and expressing feelings about one's problems and solutions
4. Environmental reevaluation. Assessing how one's problems affect the physical environment
5. Helping relationships. Being open and trusting about problems with someone who cares
6. Stimulus control. Avoiding stimuli that are associated with problem behaviors
7. Counter-conditioning. Substituting alternatives for problem behaviors
8. Social liberation. Increasing alternatives for nonproblem behaviors
9. Self-reevaluation. Assessing how one feels and thinks about oneself with respect to a problem
10. Reinforcement management. Rewarding oneself or being rewarded by others for making changes

According to the model, different processes are more important depending on the stage. For example, precontemplaters rarely use any of the processes, and behavioral processes are used more frequently by those in the action and maintenance stages.

The notion that substance abusers progress from stage to stage in an invariant sequence, as suggested by the Stages of Change Model, has been challenged (Sutton, 1996). Nonetheless, the Stages of Change Model does appear to provide a framework within which to conceptualize and understand change (Sutton, 1996).

At the very least, the Stages of Change Model underscores the point that recovery (whether guided by treatment intervention or not) is in some significant part dependent on the individual deciding to change or not (Davidson, 1996).

Understanding motivation to change, or lack of motivation to change, and the processes involved, holds some promise of therapeutic application—that is, interventions can be tailored according to an individual's stage of use. For example, at the precontemplation stage it may be most helpful to assist the individual in developing awareness of the problem; practical help may be more useful to someone in the action stage (Gossop, 1996). Indeed, the Stages of Change Model serves as a basis for motivational interviewing, a Rogerian-style of treatment that attempts to engage patients at their own level of motivation (see Chapters 8 and 9).

REFERENCES

Davidson, R. (1996). Motivational issues in the treatment of addictive behaviour. In G. Edwards & C. Dare (Eds.), *Psychotherapy, psychological treatments and the addictions* (pp. 173–188). New York: Cambridge University Press.

Dodgen, C. E. (1994). *What should I know about someone who abuses alcohol or other drugs?*. Holmes Beach, FL: Learning Publications.

Gossop, M. (1996). Cognitive and behavioural treatments for substance misuse. In G. Edwards & C. Dare (Eds.), *Psychotherapy, psychological treatments and the addictions* (pp. 158–172). New York: Cambridge University Press.

Jellinek, E. M. (1952). Phases of alcohol addiction. *Quarterly Journal of Studies on Alcohol, 13*, 673–684.

Jellinek, E. M. (1960). *The disease concept of alcoholism*. New Haven, CT: Hill House Press.

Keller, M. B., Lavori, P. W., Beardslee, W., Wunder, J., Drs, D. L., & Hasin, D. (1992). Clinical course and outcome of substance abuse disorders in adolescents. *Journal of Substance Abuse Treatment, 9*, 9–14.

Light, W. H. (1985). *Alcoholism: Its natural history, chemistry and general metabolism*. Springfield, IL: Charles C. Thomas.

Prochaska, J. O., & DiClemente, C. C. (1986). Toward a comprehensive model of change. In W. R. Miller & N. Heather (Eds.), *Treating addictive behaviors*: *Processes of change* (pp. 3–27). New York: Plenum Press.

Shaffer, H. J., & Robbins, M. (1995). Psychotherapy for addictive behavior: A stage-change approach to meaning making. In A. M. Washton (Ed.), *Psychotherapy and substance abuse: A practitioner's handbook* (pp. 103–123). New York: The Guilford Press.

Sutton, S. (1996). Can "stages of change" provide guidance in the treatment of addictions? In G. Edwards & C. Dare (Eds.), *Psychotherapy, psychological treatments and the addictions* (pp. 189–205). New York: Cambridge University Press.

Vaillant, G. E., Gale, L., & Milofsky, E. S. (1982). Natural history of male alcoholism: II. The relationship between different diagnostic dimensions. *Journal of Studies on Alcohol, 43*(3), 216–232.

Vaillant, G. E., & Milofsky, E. S. (1982). Natural history of male alcoholism: IV. Paths to recovery. *Archives of General Psychiatry, 39*, 127–133.

van Kalmthout, M. A. (1992). Spontaneous remission of addiction. In G. M. Schippers, S. M. M. Lammers & C. P. D. R. Schaap (Eds.), *Contributions to the psychology of addiction* (pp. 47–64). Amsterdam: Swets & Zeitlinger.

Webster's new universal unabridged dictionary. (1955). Springfield, MA: G. & C. Merriam Company.

5

PREVENTION, EARLY INTERVENTION, AND HARM REDUCTION

GENERAL PERSPECTIVE

The field of prevention of mental illness has emerged from the spirit of community psychology (Zax, 1980). The concerns driving prevention efforts include those about the effectiveness of psychotherapy with already established disorders, inequities in the distribution of available services, and shortages of mental health providers relative to the number of people needing services. The cogent point has been advanced that no epidemic has ever been eradicated only by treating those afflicted with the disease (Felner, Silverman, & Adix, 1991).

In prevention, a perspective that extends beyond the traditional individual-centered treatment approach enables more people to be helped. Generally, prevention programs have an interest in expanding the target of intervention (from the individual to larger groups—e.g., school, community) and shortening the time frame by intervening sooner rather than later. The prevention literature focuses on function, wellness, and health-promotion rather than on disability. There is an enhanced interest in the collaboration of medical professionals, as well as professional agencies, and a focus on achieving tangible results in terms of improved functioning, independence, and self-sufficiency (England & Cole, 1992).

TYPES OF PREVENTION

Preventive interventions can be discussed in terms of three dimensions: timing of intervention, target, and type of intervention. Regarding the time frame, preventive activities are described as primary, secondary, and tertiary (Caplan, 1964; discussed in Gibbs, Lachenmeyer, & Sigal, 1980).

1. Primary prevention. Primary prevention efforts attempt to stop the development of mental illness before it manifests. Implicit in primary prevention activities is the belief that causative factors can be identified and altered. Examples of primary prevention interventions for substance abuse include mass media efforts to raise awareness about social pressures that contribute to the initiation of substance use (such as those sponsored by the Partnership for a Drug Free America), as well as other educational efforts sponsored by well-known groups such as Mothers Against Drunk Driving (MADD), and Drug Abuse Resistance Education (DARE).

2. Secondary prevention. Secondary prevention programs attempt to identify those people who are at high risk to develop a substance abuse disorder and to intervene to prevent development of a full-blown disorder. This approach assumes that risk factors for substance abuse are known. A program that targets school dropouts would be an example of a secondary prevention program.

3. Tertiary prevention. Tertiary prevention interventions are designed to reduce the severity of an already existing substance abuse disorder. Essentially, tertiary prevention is represented by traditional treatment programs; a person is already fully symptomatic and treatment is undertaken to stop the progression of the disorder and rehabilitate that person.

Targets of Prevention Efforts

The possible targets of preventive interventions include a spectrum from the individual, increasing in scope to family, school, community, region, country, and so on.

Types of Interventions

The third dimension of preventive intervention involves the type of intervention— that is, what is actually done once a target group has been identified. Examples are teaching of refusal skills, education about drugs and their effects, improvement of family communication, and teaching parenting skills.

Early prevention efforts were crude and ineffective, focusing primarily on scare tactics (Hansen, 1994) or misguided educational efforts that may have actually encouraged substance abuse by raising curiosity and interest (Leukefeld & Clayton, 1994). These early disappointing efforts led to a movement toward the use of empirically tested approaches. Prevention studies and concepts that are representative of the existing literature will be discussed in seven nonmutually exclusive categories. The categories are consistent with the conventional presentation in professional journals and include supply reduction/legal interventions, risk and protective factors, skills training, community-based prevention, school-based programs, parenting/family interventions, and related risks/harm reduction. Significant overlap among these categories is noted. For example, a school-based prevention program may target high-risk students and employ social skills training as part of its intervention efforts. This program would involve the categories of risk, skills training, and school-based interventions. The organizational plan is used only to provide some structure to the literature in order to facilitate discussion and understanding.

SUPPLY REDUCTION/LEGAL INTERVENTIONS

The examination of the effects of law on consumption of alcohol includes factors such as the following (Hawkins, Catalano, & Miller, 1992):

1. Taxation. As taxes are raised, thus increasing the cost to the consumer, alcohol consumption decreases.

2. Laws to whom alcohol is sold. Reduction in the legal drinking age results in an elevation of teen drinking and driving, as well as traffic fatalities. Conversely, an increase in the legal drinking age results in a decrease in drinking and driving.

3. Laws regarding how alcohol is sold. In terms of the regulation of alcohol sales, the sale of distilled spirits by individual drink results in an increase in consumption and in the frequency of alcohol-related accidents.

4. Alteration of the minimum acceptable blood alcohol content (BAC). As the legally acceptable BAC is lowered, fewer alcohol-related fatal automobile accidents are observed.

5. Establishment of dram shop laws (i.e., laws placing liability on those who sell to customers who are later involved in alcohol-related accidents) (Hansen, 1994). Dram shop laws have resulted in a reduction of alcohol-related fatalities.

Changes in consumption of alcohol that are related to changes in the law occur for two reasons: laws reflect societal norms and attitudes (e.g., more restrictive laws reinforce community intolerance of substance abuse), and legal interventions reduce the supply of alcohol (Hawkins *et al.*, 1992). Evidence demonstrates that availability of alcohol and other illicit substances is related to consumption and abuse (Hawkins *et al.*, 1992)—that is, as alcohol and drugs are made less available, consumption and abuse decline. The relationship between reduction of supply and reduction of abuse has served as the basis for aggressive governmental activities pursuing legal sanctions for drug-related activities. It is generally accepted, however, that the supply-reduction activities of law enforcement agencies cannot alone control substance abuse (Leukefeld & Clayton, 1994).

RISK AND PROTECTIVE FACTORS

The study of risk and protective factors is significant because knowledge of variables related to the development of psychoactive substance use disorders can help to guide intervention efforts (Van Hasselt *et al.*, 1993). A risk factor for substance abuse is a condition that is associated with an increased probability of the development of a substance use disorder (Hawkins *et al.*, 1992). A protective factor for substance abuse is a condition associated with a decreased likelihood of the development of a substance use disorder (Jessor, Van Den Bos, Vanderryn, Costa, & Turbin, 1995) or, stated another way, a factor that reduces the impact of exposure to risk (Hawkins *et al.*, 1992). Protective factors are not simply the opposite of risk factors. Protective factors reduce the probability of the development of a substance abuse disorder in individuals with risk. Risk factors are thought to have an additive effect—that is, the more risk factors present in an individual, the greater the likelihood of substance abuse for that individual. Similarly, the more protective factors present, the less likely it is that the individual will succumb to risk conditions to develop a substance use disorder.

Risk Factors

As the preceding discussion indicates, preventive interventions should be designed to reduce risk factors or enhance protective factors. Hawkins and colleagues (1992) discussed risk factors in terms of two categories: broad social and cultural factors, individual and interpersonal environment.

**Broad Social and Cultural Factors Associated
with Elevated Risk of Substance Abuse**

1. Laws/norms that are more tolerant of substance abuse (e.g., legal drinking age of 18 versus 21)
2. Greater availability of substances
3. Greater economic deprivation

**Individual and Interpersonal Environmental Factors
Associated with Elevated Risk of Subtance Abuse**

1. Poor impulse control and sensation-seeking behavior
2. Genetic loading (i.e., positive family history of substance abuse)
3. Family alcohol/drug behavior and attitudes that are positive about substance use
4. Low levels of family bonding
5. Early and persistent behavior problems
6. Academic failure
7. A low commitment to school
8. Association with drug-using peers

9. Alienation from the dominant values of society
10. A positive attitude about substances
11. Premature sex and early pregnancy
12. Early onset of substance use

Protective Factors Mitigating Risk of Substance Abuse

Studies of protective factors identify the following conditions as helping to mitigate risk (Jessor *et al.*, 1995):

1. An attitude of intolerance of deviance
2. A positive orientation to school
3. A positive orientation toward health
4. Positive relations with adults
5. Having friends who model conventional behavior
6. A strong perception of regulatory controls (i.e., awareness of rules of conduct)
7. Participation in prosocial activities (volunteer activities, school clubs, etc.)

An illustrative example of how knowledge of risk and protective factors can guide prevention efforts is the Substance Use Prevention and Educational Resource II (SUPER II) study (Bruce & Emshoff, 1992). The SUPER II targeted high-risk urban youths, ages 11 to 17. This was a multicomponent, comprehensive program consisting of seven 2-hour sessions conducted with parents and children. The interventions included educational, experiential, and skill-building activities designed to change attitudes about drugs and alcohol, improve family interaction, build self-esteem, and develop drug-refusal skills. Positive results were reported in terms of improvement of parenting skills and family functioning, as well as a decrease in substance use among the children. The results of this study are consistent with the conclusion of Hawkins and colleagues (1992) that comprehensive, early, multicomponent programs that simultaneously address multiple risk and protective factors are most successful.

SKILLS TRAINING

As mentioned previously, early prevention efforts were relatively simplistic and ineffective. More recent approaches are based on a more sophisticated understanding of the etiology and initiation of substance abuse. The seminal work of Evans (1976) represented a shift from the original approaches to the focus on forces thought to be integrally linked with the initiation of cigarette use (i.e., peer influences) (Botvin, Baker, Dusenburg, Tortu, & Botvin, 1990; Shope, Copeland, Maharg, Dielman, & Butchart, 1993). Evans's work (1976), which was very effective, involved the teaching of skills to resist social influences to smoke cigarettes. Similarly, the approach of Botvin and associates (1990) targets interventions to alter social, developmental, and psychological factors associated with the initiation and early use of substances. Substance use initiation is conceptualized as the result of an interaction between many factors: social (i.e., peers, family, media), personal (e.g., self-esteem, self-efficacy), cognitive (e.g., attitudes, expectations), and behavioral (e.g., coping skills).

The Life Skills Training (LST) program teaches "cognitive-behavioral skills for building self-esteem, resisting advertising pressure, managing anxiety, communicating effectively, developing personal relationships, and assertion of personal rights" (Botvin, Schinke, Epstein, & Diaz, 1994, p. 118). The LST programs employ group discussion, modeling, behavioral rehearsal, reinforcement, and homework assignments in order to achieve the desired goals. Studies employing LST are effective in reducing substance use, increasing knowledge about substance use, and enhancing interpersonal and communication skills (e.g., Botvin *et al.*, 1990). Positive results have been demonstrated across different settings (e.g., rural, suburban, urban) and with white, African American, and Hispanic adolescents of both sexes (Botvin *et al.*, 1990).

Other programs employing approaches similar to the LST, which train subjects in social skills (Blume, Green, Joanning, & Quinn, 1994; Caplan *et al.*, 1992) and substance refusal skills (Shope *et al.*, 1993), demonstrate positive results.

COMMUNITY-BASED PREVENTION

Community-based prevention programs are extraordinarily difficult to plan, implement, and monitor because of the scope of such projects (Giesbrecht & Ferris, 1993; Lorion & Ross, 1992).

Community-level prevention efforts are founded on the following ideas (Giesbrecht & Ferris, 1993):

1. Substance abuse affects everyone.
2. Prevention interventions of broad scope may be more cost-effective than treatment of individuals.
3. Substance abuse is embedded in the context of community norms.
4. Etiological factors may be best addressed at the community level.

Cook and colleagues (Cook, Roehl, Oros, & Trudeau, 1994) presented a model for community-based intervention projects. They assert that effective prevention of substance abuse requires coordination, community-wide strategy, involvement of organizations and institutions, and use of many preventative activities over the long term. To give some appreciation for the magnitude and complexity of the model, they discussed the involvement of health services, social services, the educational system, the criminal justice system, religious organizations, and the business community in developing alternative activities, school-based programs, public media campaigns, policy changes, and neighborhood-based programs to reduce risk and enhance protective factors. Needless to say, programs of such magnitude and complexity are difficult to manage. In addition, the effectiveness of such programs is very difficult to measure.

SCHOOL-BASED PROGRAMS

School-based prevention has been described as the "workhorse" of prevention programs. Schools have the considerable advantage of possessing large numbers of children in a natural environment. School-based interventions not only involve children but also can enhance involvement of parents with the school and with other parents, reducing the isolation associated with school failure and substance abuse (Mclaughlin & Vacha, 1993). Prevention efforts are usually directed at elementary and middle-school children (grades 5 through 8). Because most substance use is initiated in adolescence, children and adolescents are the primary targets for prevention efforts.

Due to the fact that teachers and school counselors typically implement school-based programs, the importance of effective training has been underscored by researchers who note that the fidelity with which interventions are executed is highly variable (McLaughlin & Vacha, 1993; Rohrbach, Graham, & Hansen, 1993). Also, although many programs have been effective in the short-term, serious concerns about the maintenance of effects have been reported (Resnicow & Botvin, 1993). Resnicow and Botvin (1993) identified the following factors, which they thought accounted for the disappointing lack of staying power of school-based programs:

1. Insufficient dose of treatment. Regarding the dose of interventions, most programs offer approximately 10 sessions across 2 years; programs offering booster sessions over longer periods of time have demonstrated greater maintenance.

2. Insufficient implementation. Programs that have explicitly focused on teacher training have shown stronger results and higher fidelity in the implementation of program interventions.

3. Inappropriate expectations. In terms of expectations, it is posited that school-based programs alone should not be expected to be a cure-all and must be supported by efforts at home and in the community.

4. Attrition of high-risk students. Attrition of high-risk students skews results as program effects on these students are unknown.

5. Curriculum limitations. Curricular limitations stem from the fact that not everything is known about how to prevent substance abuse; more complete knowledge about the causes of substance abuse will result in more effective curricula.

6. Incorrect assumptions regarding age of onset. In terms of the timing of interventions, it is not known for certain whether intervention earlier or later than usual will enhance prevention effects.

7. Inappropriate messages of "zero tolerance." The possibility should be considered that it may be more effective and credible to instruct students to use substances responsibly rather than to advocate total abstinence.

Ethical considerations in school-based programs involve (a) consent from parents, (b) assent from children, (c) the right to withdraw, and (d) confidentiality concerns (Gensheimer, Ayers, & Roosa, 1991). Parental consent forms are an absolute necessity for program participation because the prospective participants are minors. It is noteworthy that consent forms are not returned for approximately 25 to 50% of students, so that many prospective program participants are lost. Regarding assent and voluntary withdrawal, it is highly debatable as to just how voluntary participation is when dealing with school-aged children. Also, confidentiality can be problematic in terms of keeping information acquired through a substance abuse program from nonauthorized school personnel.

PARENTING/FAMILY INTERVENTIONS

The rationale for parental/familial involvement in prevention efforts is that children's risks can be reduced, and protective factors enhanced, through the improvement of the family environment (Felner, Brand, Mulhall, & Counter, 1994; Ruch-Ross, 1992). By improving parenting skills, assisting in stress reduction, increasing support, and altering substance abuse behavior and attitudes, parents can improve the quality of their children's lives and the family environment (Felner et al., 1994).

Impediments to parental participation in prevention programs are significant and include (a) parents' lack of awareness of programs, (b) high drop-out rates, (c) the need for child care/free time, (d) the need for transportation, and (e) lack of acceptance of programs due to the existence of a negative stigma (Felner et al., 1994; Spoth & Redmond, 1994). Many of the above impediments have been overcome through work-based programs (Felner et al., 1994). As with school-based programs for children, the workplace has the advantage of having adults in a natural environment. In a study conducted by Felner and associates (1994), programs during mealtime were effective in engaging participants. Involvement of representatives from the community is essential for success. For example, school administrators, student assistance counselors, local parent networks, and other social service agencies can provide a network of resources people may otherwise have been be unaware of or unwilling to contact.

An illustrative example of a work-based intervention program is described by Felner and associates (1994). The program consisted of a parent training course implemented by members of various community organizations (thereby making such services more accessible in the future). The training course was conducted on company grounds and consisted of 24 1-hr training sessions, twice a week (spanning 12 weeks total). Skills were taught so as to enhance child discipline skills and reduce problematic parent–child interaction; to enhance positive parent–child interaction; to reduce parental stress, depression, and isolation; to expand parental knowledge of substance abuse; and to develop healthier attitudes and behavior toward substance use.

Among the significant findings was that the attrition rate for the program was very low (i.e., 16% compared to approximately 32% found with other parent-focused programs), underscoring the value of the program's easy access (Felner *et al.*, 1994). For those attending most of the sessions, significant improvements were reported in terms of parent–child interaction, reduced experience of stress and depression, and enhanced substance abuse knowledge and attitudes.

RELATED RISKS/HARM REDUCTION

Although there are many negative sequelae to the abuse of psychoactive substances, two areas have merited special attention: the substance abuse issues that relate to the spread of HIV and the dangers associated with pregnancy and adolescent mothers.

HIV and Substance Abuse

Substance abusers are involved with the spread of HIV in two ways: injection of drugs and engagement in high-risk sexual practices. For example, in 1992, 32% of all new AIDS cases were attributed to injection-drug risk factors (discussed in Siegal, Falck, Carlson, & Wang, 1995). Attempts to teach safer injection practices have achieved positive results (Siegal *et al.*, 1995; Wechsberg, Cavanaugh, Danteman, & Smith, 1994). For example, Siegal and associates (1995) successfully trained injection-drug abusers to (a) stop or reduce the frequency of needle and syringe sharing, (b) stop or reduce the sharing of paraphernalia (i.e., cookers, cotton, rinse water), (c) increase use of new, sterile injection equipment, (d) use bleach for cleaning injection equipment that is not new. These practices greatly reduce the risk of spreading the HIV.

Regarding sexual behavior and HIV transmission, gay and bisexual men who are noninjection substance abusers engage in frequent high-risk sex (i.e., unprotected anal sex) and have an elevated rate of HIV seropositivity (Paul, Stall, Crosby, Barrett, & Midanik, 1994; Paul, Stall, & Davis, 1993). Reported impediments to altering high-risk sexual behavior include (a) the perceived disinhibitory effects of drugs and alcohol, (b) the associated link between substance use and sex, (c) low self-esteem, (d) lack of assertiveness and negotiating skills, and (e) perceived powerlessness (Paul *et al.*, 1993). It appears, therefore, that a program that employs education and skill building will be necessary to assist this high-risk population to change sexual behavioral practices and reduce risk; simply educating them about the risks will not be adequate.

Pregnant Adolescents/Adolescent Mothers

Prenatal exposure to drugs and alcohol is associated with significant developmental, physical, and behavioral problems. Also, adolescent, substance-abusing mothers demonstrate impairment in decision making, tend to be less responsible, and have lowered inhibition resulting in poor parenting; there are elevated rates of child abuse and neglect in this population (Trad, 1993). Despite the critical need to engage pregnant adolescents and adolescent mothers in treatment, they remain undertreated. Young pregnant women/adolescent mothers experience the following obstacles to treatment (Finkelstein, 1994): (a) threat of legal consequences, (b) stigma, (c) personal denial of the need for treatment, and (d) lack of gender-specific treatment services (e.g., programs providing child care or residential programs for mother and child). Until these impediments are addressed, they are unlikely to seek/receive services that are surely needed.

Reducing Alcohol Consumption

The harm reduction concept has been applied to alter alcohol consumption habits. Instead of endorsing abstinence as a goal, programs have advocated controlled drinking practices based on cognitive–behavioral interventions (e.g., Marlatt, 1992). One illustrative study (Baer, Kivlahan, Fromme, & Marlatt, 1991) targeted the drinking practices of college students. Those students meeting the criteria for alcohol dependence were considered inappropriate for controlled drinking and were referred to an abstinence-based treatment program. Those students remaining in the program were treated as at risk for alcohol-related automobile accidents, unsafe sexual practices, impaired academic performance, and violent and criminal behavior (such as vandalism and date rape) due to their drinking behavior (Marlatt, 1992). Controlled drinking training yielded significant reductions in weekly alcohol consumption, and presumably in the related risks as well, that were maintained for 2 years (Baer *et al.*, 1991).

REFERENCES

Baer, J. S., Kivlahan, D. R., Fromme, K., & Marlatt, G. A. (1991). Secondary prevention of alcohol abuse with college student populations: A skills-training approach. In N. Heather, W. R. Miller, & J. Greeley (Eds.), *Self control and the addictive behaviors* (pp. 339–356). New York: Maxwell Macmillan Publishing Group.

Blume, T. W., Green, S., Joanning, H., & Quinn, W. S. (1994). Social role negotiation skills for substance-abusing adolescents: A group model. *Journal of Substance Abuse Treatment, 11*(3), 197–204.

Botvin, G. J., Baker, E., Dusenbury, L., Tortu, S., & Botvin, E. M. (1990). Preventing adolescent drug-abuse through a multimodal cognitive-behavioral approach: Results of a 3-year study. *Journal of Consulting and Clinical Psychology, 58*(4), 437–446.

Botvin, G. J., Schinke, S. P., Epstein, J. A., & Diaz, T. (1994). Effectiveness of culturally focused and generic skills training approaches to alcohol and drug abuse prevention among minority youths. *Psychology of Addictive Behaviors, 8*(2), 116–127.

Bruce, C., & Emshoff, J. (1992). The SUPER II Program: An early intervention program [OSAP special issue]. *Journal of Community Psychology*, 10–21.

Caplan, G. (1964). *Principles of preventive psychiatry.* New York: Basic Books.

Caplan, M., Weissberg, R. P., Grober, J. S., Sivo, P. J., Grady, K., & Jacoby, C. (1992). Social competence promotion with inner-city and suburban young adolescents: Effects on social adjustment and alcohol use. *Journal of Consulting and Clinical Psychology, 60*(1), 56–63.

Cook, R., Roehl, J., Oros, C., & Trudeau, J. (1994). Conceptual and methodological issues in the evaluation of community-based substance abuse prevention coalitions: Lessons learned from the national evaluation of the Community Partnership Program [CSAP special issue]. *Journal of Community Psychology,* 155–169.

England, M. J., & Cole, R. F. (1992). Prevention as targeted early intervention. *Administration and Policy in Mental Health, 19*(3), 179–189.

Evans, R. I. (1976). Smoking in children: Developing a social psychological strategy of deterrence. *Preventive Medicine, 5,* 122–127.

Felner, R. D., Brand, S., Mulhall, K. E., Counter, B., Millman, J. B., & Fried, J. (1994). The Parenting Partnership: The evaluation of a human service/corporate workplace collaboration for the prevention of substance abuse and mental health problems, and the promotion of family and work adjustment. *The Journal of Primary Prevention, 15*(2), 123–146.

Felner, R. D., Silverman, M. M., & Adix, R. (1991). Prevention of substance abuse and related disorders in childhood and adolescence: A developmentally based, comprehensive ecological approach. *Family Community Health, 14*(3), 12–22.

Finkelstein, N. (1994). Treatment issues for alcohol- and drug-dependent pregnant and parenting women. *Health & Social Work, 19*(1), 7–15.

Gensheimer, L. K., Ayers, T. S., & Roosa, M. W. (1991). School-based preventive interventions for at-risk populations: Practical and ethical issues. Paper presented at the Third Biennial Conference on Community Research and Action, Tempe, AZ.

Gibbs, M. S., Lachenmeyer, J. R., & Sigal, J. (Eds.). (1980). *Community psychology: Theoretical and empirical approaches.* New York: Gardner Press.

Giesbrecht, N., & Ferris, J. (1993). Community-based research initiatives in prevention [Supplement]. *Addiction, 88* 83S–93S.

Hansen, W. B. (1994). Prevention of alcohol use and abuse. *Preventive Medicine, 23,* 683–687.

Hawkins, J. D., Catalano, R. F., & Miller, J. Y. (1992). Risk and protective factors for alcohol and other drug problems in adolescence and early adulthood: Implications for substance abuse prevention. *Psychological Bulletin, 112*(1), 64–105.

Jessor, R., Van Den Bos, J., Vanderryn, J., Costa, F. M., & Turbin, M. S. (1995). Protective factors in adolescent problem behavior: Moderator effects and developmental change. *Developmental Psychology, 31*(6), 923–933.

Leukefeld, C. G., & Clayton, R. R. (1994). Drug prevention: The past as the future? *The Journal of Primary Prevention, 15*(1), 59–71.

Lorion, R. P., & Ross, J. G. (1992). Programs for change: A realistic look at the nation's potential for preventing substance involvement among high-risk youth [OSAP special issue]. *Journal of Community Psychology,* 3–9.

McLaughlin, T. F., & Vacha, E. F. (1993). Substance abuse prevention in the schools: Roles for the school counselor. *Elementary School Guidance & Counseling, 28,* 124–132.

Marlatt, G. A. (1992). Substance abuse: Implications of a biopsychosocial model for prevention, treatment, and relapse prevention. In J. Grabowski & G. R. VandenBos (Eds.), *Psychopharmacology: Basic mechanisms and applied interventions* (pp. 127–162). Washington, DC: American Psychological Association.

Paul, J. P., Stall, R. D., Crosby, G. M., Barrett, D. C., & Midanik, L. T. (1994). Correlates of sexual risk-taking among gay male substance abusers. *Addiction, 89,* 971–983.

Paul, J. P., Stall, R., & Davis, F. (1993). Sexual risk for HIV transmission among gay/bisexual men in substance-abuse treatment. *AIDS Educationand Prevention, 5*(1), 11–24.

Resnicow, K., & Botvin, G. (1993). School-based substance use prevention programs: Why do effects decay? *Preventive Medicine, 22,* 484–490.

Rohrbach, L. A., Graham, J. W., & Hansen, W. B. (1993). Diffusion of a school-based substance abuse prevention program: Predictors of program implementation. *Preventive Medicine, 22,* 237–260.

Ruch-Ross, H. S. (1992). The child and family options program: Primary drug and alcohol prevention for young children. OSAP Special Issue. *Journal of Community Psychology*, 39–54.

Shope, J. T., Copeland, L. A., Maharg, R., Dielman, T. E., & Butchart A. T. (1993). Assessment of adolescent refusal skills in an alcohol misuse prevention study. *Health Education Quarterly*, *20*(3), 373–390.

Siegal, H. A., Falck, R. S., Carlson, R. G., & Wang, J. (1995). Reducing HIV needle risk behaviors among injection-drug users in the midwest: An evaluation of the efficacy of standard and enhanced interventions. *AIDS Education and Prevention*, *7*(4), 308–319.

Spoth, R., & Redmond, C. (1994). Effective recruitment of parents into family-focused prevention research: A comparison of two strategies. *Psychology and Health*, *9*, 353–370.

Trad, P. V. (1993). Substance abuse in adolescent mothers: Strategies for diagnosis, treatment and prevention. *Journal of Substance Abuse Treatment*, *10*, 421–431.

Van Hasselt, V. B., Hersen, M., Null, J. A., Ammerman, R. T., Bukstein, O. G., McGillivray, J., & Hunter, A. (1993). Drug abuse prevention for high-risk African-American children and their families: A review and model program. *Addictive Behaviors*, *18*, 213–234.

Wechsberg, W. M., Cavanaugh, E. R., Dunteman, G. H., & Smith F. J. (1994). Changing needle practices in community outreach and methadone treatment [Special issue: Evaluating drug abuse interventions]. *Evaluation and Program Planning*, *17*(4), 371–379.

Zax, M. (1980). History and background of the community mental health movement. In M. S. Gibbs, J. R. Lachenmeyer, & J. Sigal (Eds.), *Community psychology: Theoretical and empirical approaches* (pp. 3–28). New York: Gardner Press.

6

SCREENING AND ASSESSMENT OF PSYCHOACTIVE SUBSTANCE USE

OVERVIEW OF THE ASSESSMENT PROCESS

Stage Models of Assessment

Assessment of psychoactive substance use can be conceptualized as a multistage process that is essentially the same for children, adolescents, and adults (Allen & Mattson, 1993; Tarter, 1990; Tarter & Hegedus, 1991). Goals of assessment are as follows (Allen & Mattson, 1993):

1. To obtain information for the development of an individualized treatment plan based on identified strengths and weaknesses
2. To match patients to appropriate interventions in situations in which a range of treatment options is available
3. To monitor progress so as to evaluate the effectiveness of treatment

Tarter (1990) and Allen and Mattson (1993) provide illustrative models, as described in order next.

Illustrative Stage Models of Assessment
of Psychoactive Substance Use Disorders

1. Tarter's model
   a. Screening. Ideally, the initial screening procedure makes it possible to detect the presence of a substance use disorder in a cost- and time-efficient manner.
   b. Comprehensive evaluation. Possible abusers are then targeted for more intense and comprehensive evaluation.
   c. Treatment planning. Treatment planning is a direct outgrowth of the comprehensive evaluation; interventions are directed to identified problem areas.
2. Allen and Mattson's model
   a. Screening. The goal of screening is to determine if a potential problem exists and requires more intensive evaluation.
   b. Diagnosis. The goal of the diagnosis phase is to determine if criteria (i.e., in accord with current versions of the *Diagnostic and Statistical Manual of Mental Disorders* (DSM) or *International Classification of Diseases* (ICD)) for a substance related disorder exist.
   c. Triage. The objective of the triage phase is to decide the appropriate setting and intensity for treatment (e.g., inpatient versus outpatient treatment and treatment schedule).
   d. Treatment planning. Treatment planning aims to establish individualized treatment goals and interventions.
   e. Outcome monitoring. Outcome monitoring addresses whether the patient requires further treatment.

Allen and Mattson (1993) underscore the positive impact that ongoing assessment can exert on treatment. The provision of objective feedback of progress can be reinforcing and can enhance motivation.

A review of the literature reveals an overwhelming number of assessment instruments used for psychoactive substance use disorders. To exhaustively review every measure is well beyond the scope of this publication. Entire catalogs exist for those who wish to obtain a complete list of available measures (for drug-related measures see Addiction Research Foundation, 1993; for alcohol-related measures see Allen & Columbus, 1995). Prior to reviewing actual assessment instruments, several points deserve discussion regarding the validity of self-report data and the psychometric properties of assessment instruments.

Validity of Self-Report Data

Most assessment measures rely on self-report. Many clinicians consider substance abusers unreliable informants; however, surprisingly, the self-report data of substance abusers is generally accurate (Skinner, 1982; Sobell, Toneatto, & Sobell, 1994) provide a comprehensive and very informative discussion of assessment considerations as well as specific assessment instruments). In fact, in comparison studies, self-report measures appear to be superior to laboratory tests in identifying potential substance abusers (Babor, Kranzler, & Lauerman, 1989; Fleming, 1993). Sobell and associates (1994) recommend, however, the employment of techniques that will enhance the validity of self-report data such as interview of collaterals, memory aids (e.g., Timeline Follow Back, discussed later in this chapter), prior treatment records, and laboratory tests. Accuracy of self-report is expected to decrease as a function of recent substance abuse, concurrent psychiatric problems, and physical and cognitive impairment. Absence of an assurance of confidentiality, and a poor relationship with the examiner also affect self-reports (Connors, 1995). If the patient is facing negative consequences (e.g., job or legal problems), denial and minimization can be expected (Skinner, 1982).

Factors Associated with Accurate Self-Report of Psychoactive Substance Use

1. The interviewee is not intoxicated or experiencing acute withdrawal.
2. A good rapport has been established with the clinician.
3. Confidentiality is assured.
4. There is an absence of cognitive, psychiatric, and organic mental impairment.
5. The self-report data are supported by outside information (and the patient is aware that other sources are being employed for verification).
6. There is an absence of job jeopardy and legal consequences.

Psychometric Properties of Assessment Instruments

Any discussion of assessment instruments inevitably involves a review of the psychometric properties of the instruments. The most relevant concepts include reliability, validity, sensitivity, specificity, and Receiver Operating Characteristics (ROC) analysis.

Reliability is a measure of consistency—that is, whether an assessment measure achieves the same result repeatedly (Anastasi, 1982). The reliability of an instrument is expressed as a reliability coefficient that falls between 0 and 1.0; the closer to 1.0, the more reliable the instrument.

Validity reflects the degree to which an instrument actually measures what it purports to measure (Anastasi, 1982). Validity coefficients are also expressed as a decimal falling between 0 and 1.0. The closer to 1.0, the more valid the instrument.

When discussing tests or measures for the identification of substance abusers, two concepts of particular importance are sensitivity and specificity. Sensitivity refers to the ability of the assessment instrument to correctly classify true cases, and specificity refers to the instrument's ability to correctly classify true noncases. A true case is a person who actually has the condition being assessed (e.g., alcohol abuse). A true noncase is a person who actually does not have the condition being evaluated. Therefore, in general terms, an effective instrument is both sensitive (detecting those who are afflicted with the condition) and specific (correctly identifying those who do not have the condition). Errors of classification are of two types: identifying a nonabuser as an abuser (false positive) and failing to identify an abuser (false negative). Sensitivity and specificity are both expressed as decimals ranging between 0 and 1.0; the closer to 1.0, the more sensitive or specific is the measure. Sensitivity and specificity are inversely related such that improvement in one tends to be at the expense of the other (Ross, Gavin, & Skinner, 1990).

Receiver Operating Characteristics (ROC) analysis is a process that attempts to maximize the overall classification accuracy of an assessment instrument by balancing sensitivity and specificity and identifying the best cutoff score. That is, when using an assessment instrument, a cutoff score is employed, which represents the threshold above which someone will be considered a case. For example, Ross and associates (1990) conducted a study involving the Michigan Alcohol Screening Test (MAST) (Selzer, 1971) in order to evaluate its diagnostic validity. Several cutoff scores are discussed for illustrative purposes. On the MAST, a point is scored for each alcohol-abuse-indicating response. In this study, at a cutoff of 0/1, sensitivity was 1.0 and specificity was .24. At a cutoff of 5/6, sensitivity was .98 and specificity was .57. At a cutoff of 12/13, sensitivity was .93, specificity was .76. At a cutoff of 20/21, sensitivity was .85 and specificity was .80. ROC analysis identified the cutoff of 12/13 as the optimum cutoff score to maximize selection accuracy. A few trends are worth noting. As the cutoff was raised, the sensitivity decreased. In other words, with a cutoff of 0/1, where almost everyone would be identified as an alcohol abuser, all abusers would be identified. However, many nonabusers would be incorrectly identified (false positives) as evidenced by a specificity of only .24. As the cutoff score is raised, more indicators of abuse must be present before someone is identified as an abuser. As a result, the specificity is increased—that is, fewer nonabusers are incorrectly identified as evidenced by a specificity of .80 at a cutoff of 20/21. The trade-off is a loss in sensitivity (and corresponding increase in false negatives). The ROC analysis is necessary in order to identify the optimum cutoff to achieve a balance of specificity/sensitivity and maximum accuracy of identification.

The identification of acceptable levels of sensitivity and specificity is not a simple matter. The costs and benefits of case selection must be assessed. The risks of misclassification in either direction merits careful consideration. For example, in a treatment setting it may be considered acceptable to overidentify potential treatment cases with a screening instrument with very high sensitivity and relatively low specificity in order to capture most true cases. The decision may be very different if a screening instrument is used in the criminal justice system or the workplace. The potential consequences of misclassification can be extreme (e.g., violation of parole, loss of job). In the latter two settings, it may make more sense to use a cutoff score maximizing specificity (and allowing fewer incorrect classifications of non-abusers)—that is, minimizing false positives. When considering assessment instruments it is also wise to consider the cost of the instrument, time for administration and scoring, and training necessary to administer, score, and interpret the results.

A discussion of assessment instruments commonly employed in clinical and research settings follows. The instruments are presented here in terms of their role in the assessment process (screening measure, diagnostic measure, etc.) and are also separated into two groups (alcohol and drug abuse assessment measures), as is the convention. Original references are provided for the reader interested in reviewing instruments in their entirety.

ALCOHOL SCREENING INSTRUMENTS

Michigan Alcohol Screening Test (MAST)

The Michigan Alcohol Screening Test (MAST) (Selzer, 1971) is perhaps the most widely used alcohol screening measure. The MAST is a 25-item structured interview instrument. Questions are posed in a "yes-no" response format. The measure is appropriate for use with adults and takes approximately 5 to 10 min to administer. The content of the questions relates to the experience of adverse consequences of alcohol use including medical, interpersonal, and legal difficulties. Examples of questions include the following:

1. "Have you ever been told you have liver trouble? Cirrhosis?"
2. "Have you ever lost friends or girl/boyfriends because of drinking?"
3. "Have you ever been arrested, even for a few hours, because of drunk behavior?" (Selzer, 1971, p. 91)

The MAST is well researched and considered to be psychometrically sound and effective as a screening device (Ross *et al.*, 1990; Selzer, 1971; Watson *et al.*, 1995).

Two shortened versions of the MAST exist, the Brief Michigan Alcohol Screening Test (B-MAST) (Pokorny, Miller, & Kaplan, 1972) and the Self-Administered Michigan Alcohol Screening Test (SMAST) (Selzer, Vinokar, & van Rooijen, 1975). The B-MAST uses 10 of the original 25 items, and the SMAST uses 13 of the original items in a self-administered format. Both shortened versions are considered adequate substitutes for the MAST when time for screening is very limited.

The wording of the MAST questions is such that it assesses lifetime experiences. Nearly every question begins with "Have you ever . . . ?" and this results in the report of lifetime experiences that may or may not have relevance for current diagnosis or treatment (Fleming, 1993).

CAGE Questionnaire

The CAGE Questionnaire (Ewing & Rouse, 1970) is a very brief, four-item measure. An interviewer asks the respondent four questions represented by the acronym CAGE:

1. "Have you ever felt you ought to *C*ut down on your drinking?"
2. "Have people *A*nnoyed you by criticizing your drinking?"
3. "Have you ever felt bad or *G*uilty about your drinking?"
4. "Have you ever had a drink first thing in the morning to steady your nerves or to get rid of the hangover? (*E*ye-opener)" (Ewing, 1984, p. 1907)

The CAGE questions are used with adolescents (16 years of age and older) and adults. The brevity and ease of administration of the CAGE make it an attractive and popular screening instrument in clinical settings (Liskow, Cambell, Nickel, & Powell, 1995). Psychometric properties are considered adequate (Ewing, 1984; Liskow, *et al.*, 1995; Mayfield, McLeod, & Hall, 1974; Watson *et al.*, 1995).

As with the MAST, the CAGE questions assess lifetime experiences. Therefore, the relevance of responses to current experiences is uncertain.

TWEAK

The TWEAK (discussed in Allen & Columbus, 1995) is similar to the CAGE; it consists of only five questions, and the name of the instrument, TWEAK, is an acronym representing the questions:

1. *T*olerance: "How many drinks can you hold?"
2. *W*orried: "Have close friends or relatives worried or complained about your drinking in the past year?"
3. *E*ye-openers: "Do you sometimes take a drink in the morning when you first get up?"
4. *A*mnesia (blackouts): "Has a friend or family member ever told you about things you said or did while you were drinking that you could not remember?"
5. *K* (Cut down): "Do you sometimes feel the need to cut down your drinking?" (in Allen & Columbus, 1975, p. 540)

The TWEAK is considered as useful an instrument as the MAST and CAGE with the advantage of assessing current problems (Sobell *et al.*, 1994).

Alcohol Use Disorders Identification Test (AUDIT)

The Alcohol Use Disorders Identification Test (AUDIT) was developed by the World Health Organization to identify adults whose alcohol consumption has become hazardous or harmful to their health (Saunders, Aasland, Babor, De La Fuente, & Grant, 1993). The AUDIT is a 10-item questionnaire requiring only about two minutes to administer by a health care professional or paraprofessional (Allen & Columbus, 1995). It is available in several languages and requires training for administration. Examples of questions from the AUDIT are as follows:

1. "How often do you have a drink containing alcohol?"
2. "How often during the last year have you failed to do what was normally expected from you because of drinking?"
3. "Have you or someone else been injured as a result of your drinking?" (Saunders *et al.*, 1993, pp. 795–797)

The AUDIT appears to be an adequate alcohol screening measure and has satisfactory psychometric properties (Sobell *et al.*, 1994). Advantages of the AUDIT include that it attempts to identify problem drinkers with mild as well as severe dependence, it emphasizes hazardous consumption and not just the negative consequences (as assessed by the MAST, for example), and it assesses current as well as lifetime use (Sobell *et al.*, 1994).

MacAndrew Alcoholism Scale (MAC)

The MacAndrew Alcoholism Scale (MAC) (MacAndrew, 1965) is a scale derived from the Minnesota Multiphasic Personality Inventory (MMPI). The MAC has been extensively researched as an instrument to distinguish those with alcohol problems from those without such problems based upon personality and attitudinal characteristics (Gripshover & Dacey, 1994; MacAndrew, 1965, 1981; Wasyliw, Haywood, Grossman, & Cavanaugh, 1993). The 49-item scale is covert; there are no direct questions about alcohol consumption and items were chosen empirically for inclusion on the scale. However, the MAC's ability to accurately discriminate groups of alcohol abusers from nonabusers has been seriously questioned (Gottesman & Prescott, 1989; Wasyliw *et al.*, 1993). The MAC may be most effective as a screening device to identify those with a vulnerability to addictive or risk-taking behavior in general. The MAC-R was developed when the MMPI was re-standardized (Butcher, Dahlstrom, Graham, Tellegen, & Daemmer, 1989).

Adolescent-Specific Scales

It is now well recognized that negative consequences, as well as other manifestations of substance abuse, may be different for adolescents than adults. Accordingly, measurement instruments have been developed specifically for adolescents.

Adolescent Alcohol Involvement Scale (AAIS)

The Adolescent Alcohol Involvement Scale (AAIS) (Mayer & Filstead, 1979) is a 14-item instrument designed to assess aspects of alcohol consumption and psychosocial consequences. Questions from the AAIS include the following:

1. "How often do you drink?"
2. "What is the greatest effect drinking has had on your life?"
3. "How do you feel about your drinking?" (Mayer & Filstead, 1979, pp. 171–173)

Respondents are required to choose among five to eight alternatives that best characterizes their response to a given question. The AAIS takes only about 5 min to administer and is considered to be psychometrically adequate.

MacAndrew Alcoholism Scale for Adolescents (MAC-A)

An outgrowth of the restandardization of the MMPI was the development of a version for adolescents, the MMPI-A (Butcher *et al.*, 1992). Two scales on the MMPI-A, the Alcohol/Drug Problem Proneness Scale (PRO) and the Alcohol/Drug Problem Acknowledgment Scale (ACK), demonstrated the ability to discriminate substance-abusing adolescents from psychiatric patients more successfully than the MacAndrew Alcoholism Scale-Revised (MAC-R) (Weed, Butcher, & Williams, 1994).

Rutgers Alcohol Problem Index (RAPI)

Another example of an adolescent-specific scale is the Rutgers Alcohol Problem Index (RAPI) (White & Labouvie, 1989). The RAPI is a 23-item self-administered screening instrument. Administration time is approximately 10 min. It assesses the negative consequences of alcohol use. Respondents are required to respond to 23 statements on a scale of 0 to 4, depending on the number of times the event has occurred over the previous 3 years. Examples of items on the RAPI include the following:

1. "Not able to do your homework or study for a test?"
2. "Noticed a change in your personality?"
3. "Was told by a friend or neighbor to stop or cut down drinking?" (White & Lebouvie, 1989, p. 33)

DRUG SCREENING INSTRUMENTS

Drug Abuse Screening Test (DAST)

The Drug Abuse Screening Test (DAST) (Skinner, 1982) is a 28-item self-report instrument explicitly based on the MAST (Selzer, 1971). It is used with adults and takes approximately 5 to 10 min to administer. The test items focus on the negative consequences of drug abuse; questions are posed in a yes–no format. Examples of questions on the DAST include the following:

1. "Do you ever feel bad about your drug abuse?"
2. "Has drug abuse ever created problems between you and your spouse?"
3. "Have you ever been arrested for possession of illegal drugs?" (Skinner, 1985, pp. 365–366)

The DAST, an instrument with good psychometric properties (Staley & El-Guebaly, 1990), is available in the original 28-item form or a shortened 20-item form.

Drug Use Screening Inventory (DUSI)

The Drug Use Screening Inventory (DUSI) (Tarter & Hedgedus, 1991) is a ___u-dimensional screening instrument designed to identify adolescents (16 years and older) and adults who have problems with alcohol or other psychoactive drugs. The time frame of assessment is the previous year. This instrument takes approximately 20 min to administer and can be administered in interview or self-administered forms. The DUSI consists of 149 yes–no items organized into 10 domains:

1. Substance use
2. Behavior patterns
3. Health status
4. Psychiatric disorder
5. Social competency
6. Family system
7. School performance/adjustment
8. Work
9. Peer relationships
10. Leisure/recreation

The DUSI identifies problem areas that require more intensive follow-up evaluation and attention in treatment. Scores are obtained for problem severity in each domain, and an overall score is derived to gauge general severity. An advantage of the DUSI is the breadth of areas surveyed to direct further evaluation and treatment. In addition, it is recommended as a useful measure for monitoring treatment changes and follow-up assessment (Tarter & Hegedus, 1991).

BIOLOGICAL SCREENING MEASURES

Biological screening methods are regularly employed for assessment of psychoactive substance abuse, especially in health care settings where they can easily be performed (Connors, 1995).

Alcohol-Specific Biological Screening Measures

Measurement of Recent Use

Regarding alcohol-specific measures, methods are available to assess recent use and long-term alcohol abuse (Salaspuro, 1994). Evidence of the recent use of alcohol is obtained via the direct measurement of alcohol, which remains present in bodily fluids for approximately 24 hr (Leigh & Skinner, 1988).

Bodily fluids used for blood alcohol testing include the following (Salaspuro, 1994; Sobell *et al.*, 1994):

1. Blood and urine. Laboratory analysis of blood and urine samples is the most commonly used method for assessing blood alcohol concentration. Results

obtained through laboratory methods are considered very accurate. Some limitations of using urine and blood samples are (a) cost, (b) lack of immediate results, and (c) the invasive nature of specimen collection (Sobell *et al.*, 1994).

2. Sweat. The measurement of blood alcohol concentration in sweat involves the sweat patch technique. A patch is worn on the body to continuously collect sweat. The technique is inaccurate and currently considered unsuitable for clinical use (Leigh & Skinner, 1988; Sobell *et al.*, 1994).

3. Saliva. Blood alcohol concentration is measured through saliva by the alcohol dipstick method (Sobell *et al.*, 1994). The dipstick consists of strips of filter paper that react to the fluid and change color according to the level of ethanol present. Reported reliability and validity are adequate, although some concern about the rate of false positive measurements is noted (Sobell *et al.*, 1994). This method has the advantage of being noninvasive, quick, and inexpensive. The dipstick method can also be used with urine and blood samples (Sobell *et al.*, 1994).

4. Breath analysis is also used to assess blood alcohol levels. Breath analysis provides an accurate measure of blood alcohol concentration. Advantages of breath alcohol testers are that they are noninvasive, inexpensive, easy to use, portable, and provide immediate feedback (Sobell *et al.*, 1994). To avoid false readings, patients should not smoke or drink for at least 15 minutes before a test. Also, because some breath alcohol testers are not specific for ethanol, some false positives may occur (e.g., among diabetics with high acetone levels) (Sobell *et al.*, 1994).

In addition to a direct assessment of alcohol levels, tests for biological markers can also be employed to assess current blood alcohol concentration. A biological marker is an abnormal result of a laboratory analysis indicating the presence of an abnormal state or condition (Salaspuro, 1994). The abnormal condition may be caused by disease or by exposure to toxic substances (such as alcohol or other substances). For example, measurement of levels of acetate (a product of oxidation of ethanol) and methanol (which accumulates in the body while it oxidizes ethanol) in blood provides estimates of current blood alcohol concentration.

Measurement of Long-Term Alcohol Abuse

Laboratory measurement of long-term alcohol abuse is achieved through the analysis of biological markers; the most commonly measured markers are the following (Allen & Litten, 1993; Salaspuro, 1994):

1. Gamma-glutamyl transpeptidase (GGT). GGT is an enzyme in the liver. Heavy exposure to alcohol for periods of at least several weeks can significantly raise blood levels of GGT. The reported half-life of GGT is approximately 26 days, so that elevated levels can be expected for approximately 1 month after initiation of abstinence. A limitation of the measurement of GGT is the lack of specificity. Many other factors can account for GGT elevation; including all forms of liver disease, obesity, gallbladder inflammation, aging, anticonvulsant and anti-

coagulant medications, and hyperthyroidism (Allen & Litten, 1993; Salaspuro, 1994).

2. Mean corpuscular volume (MCV). Mean corpuscular volume (MCV) is a measure of the average size of red blood cells (Allen & Litten, 1993; Salaspuro, 1994). Increased size of red blood cells is a marker of excessive alcohol intake. MCV is less sensitive but more specific than GGT as an indicator of long-term alcohol abuse. MCV decreases slowly so that it is difficult to differentiate current abusers from those recently abstinent. MCV can also be elevated (resulting in false positives) by deficiencies of nutrients (e.g., vitamin B12, and folate), liver disease, blood loss, aging, smoking, hypothyroidism, menopause, and anticonvulsant medications (Salaspuro, 1994).

3. Carbohydrate-deficient transferace (CDT). Carbohydrate-deficient transferace (CDT) is an abnormal variant of transferrin, a blood protein that functions in the transport of iron through the bloodstream (Salaspuro, 1994). CDT levels increase in response to alcohol consumption. CDT is considered a less sensitive marker for alcohol abuse than GGT, but more specific than GGT and MCV. False positives are caused only by rare genetic conditions and nonalcohol-related cirrhosis.

Because there is no single, ideal marker of alcohol abuse, researchers have attempted to combine the use of markers to enhance identification of alcohol abusers. No ideal combination has been identified to maintain sensitivity, specificity, and cost within acceptable ranges (Allen & Litten, 1993; Salaspuro, 1994). Some suggest that the best use of laboratory test results may be to establish a within-subject baseline that can be monitored over time for changes, indicating abstinence or continued use of alcohol depending on whether values are falling or rising (Leigh & Skinner, 1988; Sobell et al., 1994).

The use of laboratory testing and psychometric instruments together appears promising (Allen & Litten, 1993). The use of alcohol-specific self-report measures and laboratory tests can be very effective in correctly classifying harmful drinkers (e.g., Babor et al., 1989). Laboratory tests and psychometric instruments may be best thought of as complimentary techniques with different strengths and weaknesses. Several authors emphasize the potential motivation- and credibility-enhancing qualities of laboratory test results when used to support self-report data (Allen & Litten, 1993; Hoeksema & deBock, 1993; Salaspuro, 1994).

Laboratory Assessment of Drugs Other Than Alcohol

Methods of Measurement of Recent Use

Tests exist to detect recent use as well as long-term abuse.

1. Saliva. The presence of several drugs can be identified through analysis of saliva (e.g., marijuana, cocaine, phencyclidine, barbiturates, and metabolites of smoking—cotinine and thiocyanate). Analysis of saliva is considered inferior to

urinalysis because concentrations of drugs are lower in saliva and are retained for a shorter period of time than in urine. Advantages of analysis of saliva are that it is noninvasive and samples are less prone to tampering (Sobell *et al.*, 1994).

2. Hair analysis. Hair analysis is used primarily for the assessment of long-term use of substances.

3. Urine and blood analysis. Urine and blood analysis are the most common methods for detecting drugs and drug metabolites. Urine testing is preferred over blood analysis for a number of reasons: (a) it is less invasive than drawing blood, (b) large samples can be collected easily, (c) relatively high concentrations of drugs and metabolites are found in urine because of the concentrating function of the kidneys, (d) urine is easier to analyze than blood, and (e) long-term storage of positive samples is possible, allowing for follow-up testing, because drugs and metabolites are stable in frozen urine (Council on Scientific Affairs, 1987). It is important to collect urine samples under direct observation so no tampering or substitution occurs. The duration of detection of drugs in urine is well known (Council on Scientific Affairs, 1987; Schuckit, 1995).

Approximate Limits of Detection of Psychoactive Substances

1. 24 hr: Alcohol and short-acting barbiturates (e.g., secobarbital)
2. 48 hr: Amphetamine/methamphetamine and opioids (codeine and morphine)
3. 48 to 72 hr: Cocaine metabolites and intermediate-acting barbiturates (e.g., amobarbital)
4. 72 hr: Benzodiazepines and methadone
5. Up to 1 week: Long-acting barbiturates (e.g., phenobarbital) and PCP
6. Up to 4 weeks: cannabinoids

Urine screening is usually a two-stage process (Council on Scientific Affairs, 1987). Relatively inexpensive tests to detect a broad spectrum of drugs are sensitive but not sufficiently specific. Therefore a positive finding requires further analysis. Initial drug screens are usually conducted by a method called thin-layer chromatography (TLC). Screening is also done with methods based on immunoassays—that is, based on the production of antibodies to drugs. Two forms of immunoassays are enzyme-multiplied immunoassay technique (EMIT) and radioimmunoassay (RIA). The immunoassay techniques are more sensitive than the chromatography (TLC) method, but they are more costly and still require follow-up testing because of cross-reactions of various drugs. Confirming tests are conducted with the most sensitive and specific techniques such as gas chromatography and gas chromatography/mass spectrometry. These tests are costly, require specialized training and equipment, and require time to prepare samples (Council on Scientific Affairs, 1987).

Assessment of Chronic Drug Abuse

Hair analysis is employed for the detection of long-term drug abuse (Schuckit, 1995; Sobell *et al.*, 1994). Drawbacks of this method are that it is a relatively expensive technique, it does not determine recent use, and there are cross-reactions of drugs rendering the results less accurate (Sobell *et al.*, 1994).

DIAGNOSTIC INSTRUMENTS

Identification via a screening measure means that the person in question is likely to have a problem with substance use. The next step in the assessment process is to evaluate the person more intensively and provide a diagnosis. Diagnosis of a psychoactive substance use disorder usually depends on meeting the criteria referenced in a version of the DSM or ICD. Diagnoses based on these classification systems are based on the dependence syndrome first delineated with alcohol (Edwards & Gross, 1976). The essential features of the dependence syndrome are impaired control of use of a substance, tolerance, withdrawal, substance-seeking behavior, and a compulsion to use the substance. Related disorders stem from the psychosocial consequences often associated with substance abuse.

Many of the instruments used for diagnostic purposes are clinical interview scales. Some frequently used scales are discussed later. The scales can be classified as follows (Grant & Towle, 1990; Hasin, 1991):

1. Structured. Structured diagnostic interviews are designed to be administered by trained lay interviewers. The interviewer reads questions exactly as written, in a predetermined order, and records responses exactly as reported. There is no clinical judgment required and the patient determines whether or not a symptom is present. Fully structured interview formats are used most often in research studies.

2. Semistructured. Semistructured diagnostic interviews are designed to be administered by clinicians. Introductory questions about areas to be covered in the assessment are prescribed. Follow-up questions for classification and verification rely on the clinician's judgment. In these interviews the clinician is the one who decides whether a given symptom is present.

3. Unstructured. In an unstructured interview, the clinician decides which questions to ask in order to assess the presence or absence of a particular disorder.

The Alcohol Use Disorders and Associated Disabilities Interview Schedule (AUDADIS)

The Alcohol Use Disorders and Associated Disabilities Interview Schedule (AUDADIS) is a fully structured interview scale designed to evaluate alcohol use disorders, other drug use disorders, and psychiatric disorders (Grant & Hasin, 1991). The AUDADIS was designed by the National Institute on Alcohol Abuse and Alcoholism (NIAAA) to be administered by lay interviewers to adults. Its primary use is in large-scale epidemiological surveys of the general public, although clinical applications are possible. Administration time is 1 to 2 hours and requires significant training for administration. The schedule yields diagnoses in terms of DSM III, DSM III-R, DSM IV, and ICD 10.

Composite International Diagnostic Interview: Authorized Core Version 1.0 (CIDI-Core)

The Composite International Diagnostic Interview: Authorized Core Version 1.0 (CIDI-Core) was developed by the World Health Organization as a structured interview schedule available in many languages for international use (discussed in Allen & Columbus, 1995). The scale addresses criteria of DSM III-R and ICD 10 for various time frames (lifetime, last year, last 6 months, last month, and last 2 weeks). Scales exist for the assessment of alcohol and other drugs of abuse. Its primary use is for large-scale epidemiological surveys, and it can be used clinically. Administration time is 60 to 90 min.

Structured Clinical Interview for DSM III-R (SCID)

The Structured Clinical Interview for DSM III-R (SCID) (discussed in Allen & Columbus, 1995) is a semistructured interview instrument and was designed primarily for use in treatment settings to assess for Axis I, DSM III-R disorders. The SCID is a popular instrument that must be administered by a trained interviewer with clinical experience and familiarity with DSM III-R. The SCID has 115 items and takes approximately 60 to 90 min to complete (Sobell *et al.*, 1994).

Addiction Severity Index (ASI)

The Addiction Severity Index (ASI) (McLellan, Luborsky, Woody, & O'Brien, 1980) is a structured clinical interview developed for the specific assessment of drug and alcohol abuse. The ASI has been revised many times (McLellan *et al.*, 1992); it can be administered by a technician in approximately 60 minutes. It is made for administration to adults to assess seven potential problem areas of substance abuse: medical status, employment and support, drug use, alcohol use, legal status, family/social status, and psychological status. Questions address recent and lifetime events. The ASI yields two sets of scores: severity ratings (subjective rating of a patient's need for treatment) and composite scores (measurement of problem severity during prior 30 days). The ASI is primarily used to identify problem areas for treatment planning and outcome evaluation.

A version for assessment of adolescents is currently available (Teen ASI) (Kaminer, Bukstein, & Tarter, 1991).

Fagerstrom Tolerance Questionnaire (FTQ)

The most frequently used measure to assess nicotine dependence is the Fagerstrom Tolerance Questionnaire (FTQ) (Fagerstrom, 1978). The FTQ is a brief, eight-item self-report questionnaire that inquires about such specifics as morning smoking, inhalation, and number of cigarettes smoked per day. The FTQ was revised in 1991 (Heatherton, Kozlowski, Frecker, & Fagerstrom) and renamed the Fagerstrom Test for Nicotine Dependence (FTND). Both the FTQ and the FTND demonstrate good psychometric properties (Pomerleau, Carton, Lutzke, Flessland, & Pomerleau, 1994).

Clinical Institute Withdrawal Assessment–Revised (CIWA-AR)

The assessment for the presence of withdrawal symptoms has important diagnostic and treatment implications. The Clinical Institute Withdrawal Assessment-Revised (CIWA-AR) (Sullivan, Sykora, Schneiderman, Naranjo, & Sellers, 1989) is an eight-item scale used to assess adults for alcohol withdrawal symptoms based upon DSM III-R criteria. It can be administered by a nonprofessional or professional in several minutes. The scale yields a score indicating the severity of alcohol withdrawal syndrome. The results of the CIWA-AR are important for monitoring the need or effectiveness of the detoxification medication.

Knowledge of Symptoms of Withdrawal and Intoxication

Withdrawal and intoxication syndromes are classified in the DSM IV (APA, 1994) as substance-induced disorders. The evaluating clinician should be alert for signs of withdrawal from all major classes of drugs of abuse. Withdrawal symptoms can be found in DSM IV (APA, 1994), listed by drug. A summary list of withdrawal symptoms, presented by drug class, follows:

1. Central nervous system stimulants
   a. Dysphoric mood
   b. Fatigue
   c. Vivid unpleasant dreams
   d. Sleep disturbance
   e. Psychomotor retardation or agitation
   f. Increased appetite
2. Nicotine
   a. Dysphoric mood
   b. Insomnia
   c. Irritability
   d. Anxiety
   e. Impaired concentration
   f. Restlessness
   g. Decreased heart rate
   h. Increased appetite/weight gain
3. Central nervous system depressants
   a. Autonomic hyperactivity (e.g., sweating or elevated pulse rate)
   b. Hand tremor
   c. Nausea or vomiting
   d. Insomnia

     e. Psychomotor agitation
     f. Anxiety
     g. Transient hallucinations
     h. Grand mal seizures
     i. Death
4. Cannabinoids
     a. No withdrawal symptoms
5. Opioids
     a. Dysphoric mood
     b. Nausea or vomiting
     c. Muscle aches
     d. Runny eyes or nose
     e. Pupillary dilation
     f. Sweating
     g. Fever
     h. Diarrhea
     i. Insomnia
6. Hallucinogens
     a. No withdrawal symptoms

Clinicians should also be familiar with signs of intoxication for all major classes of drugs of abuse. As with withdrawal symptoms, they can be found in DSM IV. Symptoms of intoxication are discussed in Chapter 1.

Measures of Consumption of Alcohol and Other Substances

Many measures exist to estimate the amount of alcohol consumed, most of which require retrospective recall. Sobell and colleagues (1994) reviewed several approaches including lifetime drinking history (LDH), quantity-frequency (QF) methods, and the timeline follow back (TLFB) method.

Lifetime Drinking History (LDH)

The lifetime drinking history (LDH) method (discussed in Allen & Columbus, 1995) was developed to illustrate the distinct phases and changes in a person's lifetime drinking patterns. It provides an overview of drinking patterns and life event changes. The LDH is a structured interview applicable to adults and adolescents and takes about 20 min to administer. A limitation of the LDH is that detailed information about recent drinking is not gathered by this approach (Sobell *et al.*, 1994).

Quantity–Frequency Methods (QF)

Quantity–frequency (QF) methods assess the average number of drinks consumed per day of drinking and the frequency of drinking within a specified time frame. The many versions of QF methods are also known as estimation formulae. An example of a QF assessment device is the Composite Quantity–Frequency Index (discussed in Allen & Columbus, 1995). Examples of questions include the following:

1. "During the past 30 days how often did you drink beer?"
2. "How much beer did you drink on a typical day (in which you drank beer) during the past 30 days?" (Allen & Columbus, 1995, p. 457)

QF methods are easy and brief to administer, and they are effective in establishing typical patterns of alcohol consumption. However, the QF methods are unable to detect problematic drinking during atypical days or particularly heavy drinking (Allen & Columbus, 1995; Sobell *et al.*, 1994).

Timeline Follow Back (TLFB)

Timeline follow back (TLFB) is a method of drinking estimation that attempts to obtain detailed information about daily alcohol use through the employment of various memory aids (Sobell *et al.*, 1994). The aids include the following:

1. Daily calendar
2. Key dates (holidays, birthdays, personal events)
3. Standard drink conversion
4. Black and white days (i.e., significant periods of light or heavy drinking)
5. Discrete events and anchor points (e.g., arrests, illnesses, employment)
6. Boundary procedure (establishing highest and lowest drinking periods)
7. Exaggeration technique (a technique to more accurately quantify number of drinks; for example, "You said you drank a lot of beer. Is a lot five or 50?")

The TLFB method can evaluate drinking behavior with time frames up to 1 year. Time of administration varies depending on the length of time assessed; approximately 30 min are needed to cover a 12-month time frame. The TLFB can be self-administered or administered by a clinician. Advantages stem from the detailed estimation of drinking behavior, which allows for analysis of patterns, such as relapse triggers, and antecedents and consequences of heavy drinking (Sobell *et al.*, 1994).

Self-Monitoring

Finally, self-monitoring is a method of assessing alcohol use typically in the form of logs or diaries (Sobell *et al.*, 1994). Advantages of this approach include the accuracy of the report (it does not rely on memory) and feedback on treatment effectiveness. As with the TLFB method, detailed accounts help in the analysis of significant events such as relapse. Limitations include the fact that some patients do not comply with prescribed recording of their alcohol use. Also, historical information is not obtained through this method (Sobell *et al.*, 1994).

Measurement of drug consumption is not as straightforward as measurement of alcohol consumption for several reasons: (a) users are not always aware of the strength or concentration of drugs they are using; (b) because many drugs of abuse are illegal, the accuracy of reporting is questionable; and (c) various routes of administration will alter blood levels of a given drug (Sobell *et al.*, 1994). An example of a drug history questionnaire was presented by Washton (1995). The abuser is asked to report his or her use history for all major drugs of abuse. The questionnaire inquires about the following:

1. Age at first use
2. Age of peak use
3. Routes of administration
4. Typical amount of substance used on a day of use
5. Date of last use

The timeline follow back (TLFB) method can also be employed with substances other than alcohol, as can the self-monitoring techniques (Sobell *et al.*, 1994).

Knowledge of High-Risk Groups

For diagnostic purposes, it is helpful for the clinician to be aware of high-risk groups. Johnson (1991) identified factors associated with high-risk youth according to an Anti-Drug Abuse Act:

1. Child of a substance abuser
2. School dropout
3. Precocious sexual intercourse/early pregnancy
4. Economic disadvantage
5. Has committed a violent or delinquent act
6. Has experienced mental health problems
7. Has attempted suicide
8. Became disabled by injuries
9. Has experienced physical, sexual, or psychological abuse
10. Cigarette smoking (Johnson *et al.*, 1990)
11. Peer use of substances (Johnson *et al.*, 1990)

Due to the significant link between the experience of trauma, substance abuse, and other forms of psychopathology (Hien & Levin, 1994; Triffleman, Marmer, Delucchi, & Ronfeldt, 1995; Zaslav, 1994), assessment of traumatic experiences can aid in the diagnostic process. The Traumatic Antecedents Questionnaire (TAQ) (Herman, Perry, & van der Kolk, 1989) is a 100-item, semistructured instrument that explores childhood trauma and family environment up to age 16. The TAQ assesses the degree of exposure to five dimensions of trauma, including loss/separation, physical abuse, witnessed violence, sexual abuse, and emotional neglect.

Knowledge of Diagnostic Criteria

Assessment for the purpose of rendering a formal diagnosis requires specific knowledge of the diagnostic criteria. DSM IV (American Psychiatric Association, 1994) diagnostic criteria are summarized here. Substance dependence is manifested by three or more of the following (which must occur in the same 12-month period):

1. Tolerance
2. Withdrawal
3. The substance is taken in larger amounts or over a longer period of time than intended.
4. There is a persistent desire for the substance or unsuccessful efforts to cut down or control use.
5. A great deal of time is spent obtaining, using, or recovering from use of the substance.
6. Important activities are given up or reduced.
7. There is continued use despite knowledge that use causes or worsens psychiatric or physical conditions.

It is noteworthy that tolerance and withdrawal are no longer considered necessary or sufficient conditions for a diagnosis of substance dependence—that is, a diagnosis of substance dependence may be made with the presence of any three of the remaining criteria; if tolerance and withdrawal are present, there still must be an additional criterion symptom present in the individual in order for he or she to be diagnosed with substance dependence.

There are two specifiers applied to the diagnostic category of substance dependence: with physiological dependence (tolerance or withdrawal are observed) and without physiological dependence (no evidence of tolerance or withdrawal exists).

There are six course specifiers applied to the diagnostic category of substance dependence. Four of the six course specifiers are remission specifiers. The remission specifiers classify remission with respect to two axes: duration of remission (early or sustained remission) and degree of remission (partial or full remission). Remission specifiers can only be applied after no criteria for dependence or abuse have been met for at least 1 month and do not apply if an individual is on agonist therapy (e.g., methadone) or in a controlled environment (e.g., in prison). Remission specifiers are described as follows.

1. Early full remission. For at least 1 month, but less than 12 months, no criteria for dependence or abuse are present.
2. Early partial remission. For at least 1 month, but less than 12 months, one or more criteria for dependence or abuse are present but the full criteria for dependence have not been met.
3. Sustained full remission. No criteria have been met for dependence or abuse for 12 months or longer.

4. Sustained partial remission. The full criteria for dependence have not been met for a period of 12 or more months, but one or more criteria for dependence or abuse have been met.

The two remaining specifiers for substance dependence are the following:

5. On agonist therapy. The individual is receiving a prescribed agonist (e.g., methadone) and no criteria for dependence or abuse are present for that class of medication.
6. In a controlled environment. The individual is in an environment where access to substances is blocked (prison, hospital, etc.) and no criteria for dependence or abuse are present.

The diagnosis of substance abuse is indicated by one or more of the following occurring within a 12-month period:

1. Recurrent substance use resulting in a failure to fulfill major role obligations at work, school, or home
2. Recurrent substance use in situations that are physically hazardous
3. Recurrent substance-related legal problems
4. Recurrent substance use despite the experience of social/interpersonal problems caused or exacerbated by the substance use

Additionally, it is necessary for a diagnosis of substance abuse that the criteria for substance dependence never have been met for a given class of drug; substance dependence is a lifetime diagnosis.

AREAS TO ASSESS FOR TREATMENT PLANNING PURPOSES

In addition to performing an assessment for the purpose of diagnosis, assessment of other areas can guide treatment interventions including neuropsychological screening, expectancy measures, motivation scales, instruments to assess relapse factors/risk, and assessment of family functioning.

Neuropsychological Screening

Impairment in neuropsychological functioning is a well-recognized consequence of substance abuse (Grant, 1987; Parsons & Farr, 1981). Assessment for the presence and severity of impairment is important for documenting consequences, guiding treatment interventions, and measuring progress in recovery (Grant, 1987; Sobell et al., 1994). Observed deficits from alcohol abuse include problems in abstraction-ability/concept formation, perceptual and perceptual-motor impairment, and memory impairment (Grant, 1987). The abuse of other substances is also associated with problems in visuospatial abilities, memory, and abstract reasoning (Parsons & Farr, 1981). It is important to note that observed neuropsychological impairment is often temporary and slowly recovers for as long as a year following initiation of abstinence. The effects of substance abuse on the brain vary not only according to the amount of drug use, but also according to age, premorbid intelligence, family history of substance abuse, neuromedical history (e.g., history of head injury), education, pattern of recent substance abuse, and time of assessment relative to the initiation of abstinence (Grant, 1987).

Because neuropsychological impairment may limit a patient's ability to benefit from psychotherapeutic interventions, it is advisable to screen for such problems. Some tools that may be used for purposes of neuropsychological screening are the Mini-Mental State Exam (Folstein, Folstein, & McHugh, 1975), the Trail-Making Test (Reitan, 1979), the Benton Visual Retention Test (Benton, 1974), and subtests from the WAIS-R (Wechsler, 1981), including Block Design, Arithmetic, and Digit Symbol (Sobell *et al.*, 1994).

The Mini-Mental State Exam is a brief neuropsychological screening instrument that is heavily loaded for verbal skills. Patients are tested in five general areas including orientation, immediate recall, attention and calculation, recall, and language.

Discussion of results of neuropsychological assessment with patients can be particularly motivating (Allen & Litten, 1993).

Expectancy Measures

Expectancy measures are designed to assess a patient's expectations of effects of a substance. Expectations are related to consumption so that those expecting a positive consequence from using a given substance are likely to use the substance. Conversely, those expecting a negative consequence from using a given substance are less likely to use that substance. It is thought, therefore, that interventions targeting attitudes, expectations, and beliefs can alter consumption (Sobell *et al.*, 1994). Examples of expectancy measures include the Alcohol Expectancy Questionnaire (AEQ) (Brown, Christiansen, & Goldman, 1987) and the Marijuana Expectancy Questionnaire (Schafer & Brown, 1991). Essentially, the questionnaires provide statements about perceived benefits of a given substance and the respondent is asked to agree or disagree with each statement. Positive expectancies are inversely related to treatment outcome; an expectancy of tension reduction is highly associated with relapse (Allen & Litten, 1993).

Assessment of Motivation for Change

A scale designed to assess motivation for change is the Readiness to Change Questionnaire (RTCQ) (Rollnick, Heather, Gold, & Hall, 1992). The scale is a 12-item questionnaire that assesses stages of change based on the model designed by Prochaska and DiClemente (1986) (discussed in detail in Chapters 4 and 8). Readiness to change is viewed as a dynamic state that can be altered (Sobell *et al.*, 1994). Interventions are designed to enhance motivation for change.

Assessment of High-Risk Situations

Identification of high-risk situations for use of substances and improvement of coping in these situations are integral to recovery (especially relapse prevention). Examples of scales developed to assess high-risk situations are the Inventory of Drinking Situations (IDS) (Annis, 1986) and the Inventory of Drug Taking Situations (IDTS) (Annis, Martin, & Graham, 1992) (discussed in Allen & Litten, 1993; Sobell *et al.*, 1994). Respondents are asked to rate different situations according to the frequency with which they drank alcohol or used substances in the previous year.

Two other related measures designed by Annis and colleagues attempt to assess the subjective sense of the abuser to manage high-risk situations: the Situational Confidence Questionnaire (SCQ) (Annis, Graham, & Davis, 1987) and the Drug Taking Confidence Questionnaire (DTCQ) (discussed in Sobell *et al.*, 1994). With the SCQ and DTCQ, situations of high risk are identified and the respondent is asked to rate his or her confidence in his or her ability to resist use of a substance on a 6-point scale. These tools help guide high-risk management and relapse prevention (Allen & Litten, 1993).

Assessment of Family Functioning

It is important to examine family functioning to determine influences that contribute to risk of substance abuse or provide a therapeutic resource for treatment (Tarter, 1990). Tarter (1990) has recommended the use of a three-part instrument, the Family Assessment Measure, which yields a comprehensive profile of the family unit. The Family Assessment General Scale assesses family functioning from a systems perspective. This general scale yields an overall index and scores on seven dimensions including task accomplishment, role performance, communication, affective expression, involvement, control, and values and norms. The Dyadic Relationship Scale evaluates the quality of relationships between specific family members. The Self-Rating Scale assesses the individual's perception of his or her functioning in the family unit.

Awareness of Common Family Dynamics

Although employment of psychometric assessment tools may be helpful, it can also be advantageous for a clinician to be alert to certain family dynamics and problems that are frequently present in substance abuse cases; identification and skillful handling of these dynamics is often necessary for a successful treatment outcome. Substance abuse is frequently referred to as a "family disease." The devastating effects of having a substance abusing family member are varied and many. Three different levels of family issues deserve specific discussion: children of substance abusers, parents of substance abusers, and spouses of substance abusers.

To understand the harmful effects that a substance-abusing parent can have on his or her children, it is helpful to consider the needs of developing children.

To develop normally, all children need to be fed, cleaned, kept warm, and sheltered from physical harm. In addition, they need to feel loved, respected, valued, and important. Children need to be taught basic rules of conduct and self-control. It is vitally important for children to trust their caretakers to reliably provide what they need. In short, a child's relationship with his or her parents is the prototype for all later relationships. That is, if the parent-child relationship is generally positive and characterized by love, respect and careful attention, the child will grow to feel loved, respected, and confident. Further, the child will expect others, and the world in general, to be generally positive and satisfying. Conversely, if a child is treated as a nuisance, in an environment of neglect or minimal concern, the child will not only think poorly of him- or herself, but will expect others to behave in uncaring ways.

Fortunately, most parents adequately provide the essentials for the normal development of their children. If however, the typical behavior of substance-abusing adults is considered, it is plain to see how a situation can occur in which children's needs will not be consistently met. To the degree that the parent is experiencing psychosocial impairment, he or she will be less available to provide materially and emotionally to the family. In cases of more severe substance abuse, it is not unusual for a substance-abusing parent to stay out until the late hours of the night and to come home only to sleep, to eat, or to shower and change clothes. Or, if home, the substance-abusing parent is totally preoccupied and self-absorbed, if not in conflict with someone in the family. Obviously, a parent who is intoxicated, absent, or preoccupied is not someone who is in a position to provide to children. It should be no surprise, then, that children of substance-abusing parents often do not get what they need for normal, healthy adjustment to life. These unfortunate children grow to expect others to be untrustworthy, self-centered, and often hurtful; they usually think very little of themselves. Needless to say, someone whose self-esteem is low and who expects disappointment and unpleasant behavior from others is predisposed to maladjustment.

The effects of inadequate parenting as described are long-lasting and difficult to reverse or correct. It has been well documented that adult children of alcoholics (ACOAs) have identifiable difficulties and deficiencies. The degree of damage to a child depends on several factors including (a) the age range of the child when the parent is abusing the substance(s) (and acting in destructive ways with respect to the development of the child), (b) the level of impairment of the abusing parent, (c) the general maturity level of the child, and (d) the presence or absence of other stable parental figures for the child.

The effect of substance-abusing children on parents is also worthy of consideration. Stated simply and directly: abuse of a substance by a child is the emotional equivalent of abuse of the parents. Most parents can name no greater source of pain than to observe their child destroying him- or herself with drugs and alcohol. When one considers that a primary role of parenting is to prepare children to be happy, productive, successful members of society, substance abuse is perceived as evidence of failure as parents. Adolescent and young adult abusers often attempt to deny this by stating "I am taking drugs myself—it has nothing to do with my parents." That a child could abuse him- or herself without hurting his or her parents is simply untrue in most cases. Whether or not the substance-abusing children want to admit it, on some level they are sending a message about how they feel about themselves and their parents; it is not a message of love.

Many abusers may be unaware of the effect they are having on their parents because they simply ignore concerns expressed by their parents, are too impaired to understand their own behavior, or their parents do not express their concerns to the substance-abusing child (usually for fear that it would make matters worse). Whatever the situation, it is very important that substance-abusing children learn about the effects their behavior is having on their family. If the child cares that he or she is distressing his or her parents, this knowledge can act as a deterrent to further abuse and as a motivation to seek and remain in treatment. If the child does not care that he or she is negatively affecting the family as well as him- or herself, then this response should be investigated in treatment.

Spouses of substance abusers are often placed in a difficult-to-escape bind. On the one hand they are caretakers of the substance abuser (as well as the rest of the family) and can derive satisfaction from this role. On the other hand, they are often derogated and devalued by the substance-abusing spouse. Ambivalence about treatment among spouses of substance abusers is well recognized. In the extreme is the so-called codependent spouse. The codependent is someone whose senses of security, esteem, and well-being are attached to the receipt of approval or disapproval from the substance abuser. If approved of by the abuser, the spouse feels good and secure; if disapproved of, the spouse has the opposite experience. Unfortunately, such a codependent spouse will not consistently support treatment because he or she cannot risk their spouse's disapproval; the person may act to please the spouse, which can mean going against treatment.

Whether the child, parent, or spouse of a substance abuser, it is clear that involvement with an abuser is difficult and often harmful; treatment is usually necessary. Identification of impaired and suffering family members should be a regular component of the assessment process.

Illustrative Example and Discussion of a Complete Psychosocial/Substance Use Assessment Form

Therapists often adapt forms employed as part of intake procedures in hospitals, outpatient substance abuse and mental health treatment programs, and other clinical settings for their own assessment purposes. These unpublished assessment forms are not formal psychometric assessment measures but may provide an effective and time-efficient means of obtaining the necessary information to render a valid psychiatric/substance abuse diagnosis and to serve as a basis for initial treatment planning.

The following example of a psychosocial/substance use assessment form was used by one of the authors (C. E. D.). The categories assessed on the form derive from multiple sources including psychiatric hospital intake forms, standard mental status questions, standard substance use assessment questions, and publications (e.g., please see Othmer & Othmer, 1994, and Strub & Black, 1985, for more comprehensive discussions of psychodiagnostic interviewing). It has been our experience that clinicians in training or those practicing with relatively little experience may be familiar with assessment forms similar to the one presented but may be uncertain about how to obtain the desired information or the relevance of the information to the assessment process. For these reasons, following the presentation of the assessment form is a discussion of specific questions that may be posed to ascertain information to complete the form as well as the rationales for the inclusion of items on the form.

Presentation of the Assessment Form

Psychosocial/Substance Use Assessment Form

Name: _____

Date: _____

Age: _____

DOB: _____

S.S. #: _____

Address: _____

Phone Numbers: _____

Chief Complaint: _____
_____
_____
_____
_____

History of Present Illness: _____
_____
_____
_____
_____
_____

Educational History: _____
_____
_____
_____

Vocational History: _____
_____
_____

Developmental History: _____
_____
_____

Social/Interpersonal History: _____

_____

_____

Sexual History: _____

_____

_____

Family of Origin: _____

_____

_____

_____

Current Family: _____

_____

_____

_____

_____

Psychiatric/Psychological Treatment History: _____

_____

_____

Family Psychiatric/Psychological Treatment History: _____

_____

_____

Major Medical History: _____

_____

_____

Head Injury/Accidents: _____

_____

_____

Substance Use:

    List all substances used (including nicotine): _____

_____

    Age of first use for each substance:_____

_____

    Routes of administration for each substance: _____

_____

    Age of peak use, and amount used, for each substance: _____

_____

    Number of days of current use of each substance per week: _____

_____

    Amount of each substance used on a typical day of use: _____

_____

    Date of last use of each substance: _____

_____

    Negative consequences (problems with family, marriage, friends, work,
the law, physical health, mental health, finances, or
religion/spirituality):

_____

_____

Dangerous Behavior: _____

Presence of Symptoms of Severe Disturbance (hallucinations/delusions/bizarre behavior): _____

Obsessive-Compulsive Rituals; Tic Behaviors: _____

Mood: _____

Anxiety: _____

Significant Losses: _____

Memory: _____

Orientation: _____

Judgment: _____

Observations:

    Level of Consciousness: _____

    Affect: _____

    Appearance and Behavior: _____

    Content and Form of Thought: _____

    Language: _____

Initial Diagnostic Impression: _____

Initial Treatment Plan: _____

_____
Signature and Date

Examples of Specific Questions to Ask and Rationales for Inclusion of Items on the Assessment Form

1. Categories 1 through 7 allow for the recording of basic identifying information.
2. Chief complaint
   a. Example of a question to ask
      (1) What brings you here?
   b. Rationales for assessment of this item
      (1) Obtain description of the problem as perceived by the patient
      (2) Assessment of insight. The person who recognizes he or she is experiencing problems and can identify probable causes will be better able to cooperatively engage in the treatment process.
3. History of present illness
   a. Examples of questions
      (1) How long have you experienced these problems?
      (2) What have you done (currently and in the past) to resolve these difficulties?
   b. Rationales for assessment of this item
      (1) A longitudinal perspective is necessary to accurately assess psychoactive substance use as well as other psychiatric disorders. For example, someone may present as severely depressed on evaluation; a review of their history is necessary to determine whether their current presentation is a representative of bipolar disorder, unipolar depression, or a symptom of amphetamine withdrawal, to name several possible causes.
      (2) Efforts made to resolve difficulties give some idea of coping skills and motivation to help self or to seek assistance for problems
4. Educational history
   a. Examples of questions
      (1) How far did you go in school?
      (2) What kind of a student are/were you?
      (3) Any history of child study team involvement or receipt of special services or placement?
      (4) Any behavior problems in school? Ever suspended? Expelled?
   b. Rationale for assessment of this item
      (1) A major demand of childhood is to attend and perform at school. Difficulties adequately meeting academic demands can indicate a learning disability, intellectual deficiency, attentional problems, emotional or behavioral problems. Generally speaking, a good educational history is associated with positive adjustment and is a prognostically favorable sign.

5. Vocational history
   a. Examples of questions
      (1) Are you currently working? If so, what kind of work do you do. If not, how do you support yourself?
      (2) Do you like your work?
      (3) Have you ever been terminated from a job or experienced significant problems? If so, what kinds of problems did you experience?
      (4) Have you ever experienced extensive periods of unemployment or underemployment?
      (5) Have you ever received disability benefits? If so, what for?
   b. Rationales for assessment of this item
      (1) A major demand of adulthood is to work. Similar to educational history, a solid work history is prognostically favorable and an indicator of a person's general adjustment to life. For example, someone who is currently employed and has been so continuously for the past 5 years is functioning more effectively than someone receiving disability benefits for the past year.
      (2) Current employment status has significant implications for scheduling of treatment as well as ability to pay for treatment.
6. Developmental history
   a. Examples of questions
      (1) Are you aware of having experienced any significant delays or abnormalities in terms of achievement of developmental milestones: Sitting-up? Crawling? Standing? Walking? Talking? Toilet Training? Separation for school?
   b. Rationale for assessment of this item
      (1) Significant developmental delays are associated with developmental disorders, behavioral, intellectual, emotional, and neurological problems.
7. Social/interpersonal history
   a. Examples of questions
      (1) Are you currently socially active? If so, what kinds of things do you do with friends? If not, have you ever been socially active?
      (2) Do you have any close friends with whom you can discuss almost any topic?
      (3) Growing up, did you like other children? Did they like you?
      (4) Are you able to make and maintain long-term relationships?
   b. Rationales for assessment of this item
      (1) Inability to engage in satisfying, healthy, and long-lasting relationships is a sign of serious maladjustment.
      (2) A solid social network is a very significant aid to treatment of mental and physical maladies. If a supportive social network is lacking, it often must be provided in treatment. For example,

someone with an advanced psychoactive substance use disorder who has alienated family and friends requires the considerable social support offered in group-based treatment or Narcotics Anonymous (NA)/Alcoholics Anonymous (AA) networks.

8. Sexual history
   a. Examples of questions
      (1) What is your sexual orientation?
      (2) How old were you when you began dating?
      (3) Are you sexually active? If so, do you practice safe sex regarding disease protection? Pregnancy? How old were you at the time of first sexual intercourse?
      (4) Describe you longest continuous relationship?
      (5) Have you ever been a victim of sexual abuse?
      (6) Have you ever experienced any sexual difficulties?
      (7) Do you engage in any unusual sexual behaviors?
   b. Rationales for assessment of this item
      (1) Sexual behavior is often disturbed by substance abuse. More specifically, with frequent substance use, sex drive usually diminishes.
      (2) Disease transmission among substance abusers is a serious health risk.
      (3) Victims of sexual abuse are at elevated risk for various forms of psychopathology.
      (4) The ability to engage in long-term sexual relationships is a developmental challenge starting in adolescence. How successful one is in negotiating this developmental challenge offers another gauge of overall developmental progress/adaptation.
      (5) Sexual perversions can be a source of shame and discomfort. Direct questioning allows for a rare opportunity to discuss these very private matters that may otherwise not be reported.

9. Family of origin
   a. Examples of questions
      (1) Do you have any siblings? If so, what are their names and ages? How do you get along with them? If any are deceased, what did they die of?
      (2) Are your parents alive? If not, when and what did they die of? If alive, how old are they? Describe your mother; your father.
   b. Rationales for assessment of this item
      (1) Positive family relationships are correlated with good physical and mental health and are an asset to recovery for someone with psychosocial difficulties.
      (2) If family members are deceased, cause of death provides information about risk factors for illness for the individual being assessed.

10. Current family
    a. Examples of questions
        (1) What is your marital status? If married, how long have you been married? How would you characterize the marital relationship? If divorced, what factor(s) contributed to the divorce?
        (2) Do you have any children?
        (3) Has there ever been any violence in the home?
    b. Rationales for assessment of this item
        (1) Makeup and quality of current family life provides an indicator of a person's ability to establish and maintain a satisfying heterosexual relationship in marriage, parenting ability, and responsibility toward his or her family. Especially in cases of substance abuse, deterioration in marital and family relationships are observed.
        (2) Inquiries about violent behavior are directly made to assess for the presence of potentially dangerous behavior and the risk of its occurrence.
11. Psychiatric/psychological treatment history
    a. Examples of questions
        (1) Have you ever received mental health or substance abuse treatment services by a psychiatrist, psychologist, social worker, physician, or some other type of counselor? If so, what were you treated for? What kind of services did you receive? Was medication prescribed? Did you find the treatment helpful? How did you decide to stop treatment if it is not currently under way?
    b. Rationale for assessment of this item
        (1) Treatment history offers diagnostic and prognostic information, as well as information relevant to treatment planning. Diagnostically, if someone presenting for treatment previously received treatment for a psychiatric or substance-use disorder, the evaluating clinician should be particularly alert for the reoccurrence of the same condition(s). Prognostically, previous response to treatment will give the clinician some expectation of the current response to treatment. Finally, the current treatment plan should be guided in part by the past response to treatment—that is, those elements helpful in previous treatment should be employed in current treatment; those not helpful should be altered in the current treatment. Changes should be considered with respect to modality of treatment (e.g., individual, group, family), type of therapy (e.g., cognitive–behavioral, psychodynamic), intensity of services (number of hours of contact per week), and type of program (e.g., NA/AA, outpatient substance abuse program, partial hospitalization program).

12. Family psychiatric/psychological treatment history
    a. Examples of questions
       (1) Has anyone in your family ever received mental health or substance abuse services by a psychiatrist, psychologist, social worker, physician or any other type of counselor? If so, what were they treated for and what type of treatment did they receive?
    b. Rationale for assessment of this item
       (1) Because most, if not all, psychiatric conditions have some genetic underpinnings, the clinician is attempting to establish risk for specific psychiatric/substance use disorders.
13. Major medical history
    a. Examples of questions
       (1) Are you currently receiving medical treatment. If so, what is the nature of the illness and the treatment?
       (2) Have you experienced any significant health problems due to illness or injury?
    b. Rationales for assessment of this item
       (1) Medical conditions may be a consequence of substance abuse (e.g., respiratory infection from smoking cigarettes or marijuana).
       (2) Some medical conditions may present as psychiatric conditions. For example, diabetes and thyroid dysfunction may present as depressive disorders.
       (3) Medical conditions, especially chronic or severe illnesses, may create secondary psychiatric disorders.
       (4) Medications for the treatment of physical conditions may significantly alter cognitive, behavioral, or emotional functioning and may create psychiatric symptoms. For example, hormone replacement therapy (for menopausal women) has been observed to contribute to the experience of symptoms of depression and anxiety.
14. Head injury/accidents
    a. Examples of questions
       (1) Have you ever lost consciousness due to an accident (e.g., sporting, industrial, automobile)? If so, were there any residual changes in your thinking, emotional functioning, or behavior?
    b. Rationale for assessment of this item
       (1) A head injury with lingering effects may be the cause of psychiatric symptoms or may be a factor complicating treatment.
15. Substance use
    a. Examples of questions
       (1) The questions listed on the form are self-explanatory.
    b. Rationales for assessment of this item
       (1) These are standard questions employed to assess patterns of use and the experience of negative psychosocial consequences.

16. Dangerous behavior
    a. Examples of questions
       (1) Are you currently experiencing any thoughts or feelings about hurting or killing yourself? If yes, do you have any plans or have you engaged in any behavior? If not currently experiencing such thoughts or feelings, have you ever? Have you ever made plans or engaged in any behavior?
       (2) Are you currently experiencing any thoughts or feelings about hurting or killing anyone else? If yes, do you have any plans or have you engaged in any behavior? If not currently experiencing such thoughts or feelings, have you ever? Have you ever made plans or engaged in any behavior?
    b. Rationales for assessment of this item
       (1) Assessment for risk of suicide is necessary to determine whether steps will be necessary to protect the individual from self-harm.
       (2) Presence of risk of self-harm conveys diagnostic information, often associated with depressive conditions and character pathology.
       (3) Assessment of risk of danger to others is necessary to determine whether steps will be necessary to protect someone from the individual being assessed.
17. Presence of symptoms of severe disturbance
    a. Examples of questions
       (1) Have you ever heard voices when nobody was with you?
       (2) Have you ever seen visions of people or things that were not really present?
       (3) Have you ever felt you had special powers or abilities?
       (4) Have you ever felt people were out to get you or hurt you?
       (5) Have you ever engaged in behavior you or others would consider bizarre?
    b. Rationale for assessment of this item
       (1) Hallucinations and delusions are symptoms of severe disturbance associated with psychotic disorders and substance-related disorders.
18. Obsessive–compulsive rituals; tic behaviors
    a. Examples of questions
       (1) Have you ever experienced any involuntary muscle movements or vocalizations?
       (2) Have you ever experienced any intrusive thoughts, impulses, or images that interfere with your ability to function?
       (3) Have you ever engaged in any rituals designed to alleviate anxiety and which interfered with your ability to function?
    b. Rationale for assessment of this item
       (1) These questions are posed to directly inquire about the possible presence of symptoms of tic disorders and obsessive–compulsive disorder.

19. Mood
   a. Examples of questions
      (1) How would you describe your mood?
      (2) How is your energy level?
      (3) Are you experiencing any difficulty concentrating while doing work or reading? Are your thoughts racing?
      (4) Are you experiencing any difficulty making decisions?
      (5) Are you experiencing guilt?
      (6) Would you say that you experience low self-esteem or an inflated sense of your self?
      (7) Do you feel helpless or hopeless?
      (8) How is your sleep?
      (9) Are you experiencing any changes in appetite or weight?
      (10) Are you experiencing any changes in your motivation or interest in doing things?
      (11) Are you experiencing any thoughts or feelings of hurting or killing yourself?
   b. Rationale for assessment of this item
      (1) These are standard questions to assess for depressive and bipolar disorders.
20. Anxiety
   a. Examples of questions
      (1) Have you ever experienced anxiety characterized by sweating, palpitations, feeling lightheaded, fear of dying, or numbness/tingling?
      (2) Do you experience discomfort doing things out of the home?
      (3) Do you find it difficult to be around people?
      (4) Do you experience fear of animals or situations like being in high places or tight quarters?
   b. Rationale for assessment of this item
      (1) The above questions are employed to assess for anxiety disorders such as panic and phobic disorders.
21. Significant losses
   a. Example of a question
      (1) Have you ever experienced a loss of anybody or anything that had a significant effect on you?
   b. Rationale for assessment of this item
      (1) Poorly resolved loss has been associated with depressive disorders as well as anxiety disorders.
22. Memory
   a. Examples of questions
      (1) Can you repeat these three words now and in a minute or so from now when I ask you? (Offer respondent three words and ask for them again in 1 min).
      (2) Can you tell me what you had for breakfast today? Lunch?

   (3) Can you tell me my name?
   (4) Can you tell me today's date?
   (5) Can you tell me the name of the town you grew up in?
   (6) What is your mother's maiden name?
   (7) Who was the first president of the United States?
  b. Rationale for assessment of this item
   (1) Questions are posed to assess immediate memory (1), recent memory (2, 3, 4), and long-term memory (5, 6, 7). Memory disturbance is associated with dementing disorders, mood disorders, and disturbances of attention.

23. Orientation
  a. Examples of questions
   (1) Can you tell me today's date?
   (2) Can you tell me your name?
   (3) Can you tell me where you are right now?
  b. Rationale for assessment of this item
   (1) Disorientation or confusion is indicative of serious mental dysfunction associated with psychotic disorders, dementing disorders, or substance-related disorders.

24. Judgment
  a. Examples of questions
   (1) Questions from the WAIS-R (Wechsler, 1981), Comprehension subtest are commonly employed. For example, "What should you do if while in the movies you are the first person to see smoke and fire?" (p. 129)
  b. Rationale for assessment of this item
   (1) Impaired judgment is associated with severe psychiatric disturbance, dementing disorders, and poor impulse control.

25. Information gleaned from direct observation
  a. Level of consciousness
   (1) The examiner observes to see if the respondent is alert and able to relate to the examiner and to the environment in general. Lethargy or more severe disturbances in consciousness (obtundation or coma) not only impair the ability to conduct an interview but are indicative of organic pathology or intoxication.
  b. Affect
   (1) Affect refers to the outward expression of emotion. Affect is usually observed in tone of voice, attitude, facial expression, and body language. Affective expression is related to mood and is particularly helpful in the assessment of mood disorders, although alterations in affective functioning may also be associated with substance abuse and schizophrenia.
  c. Appearance and behavior
   (1) The examiner observes for general appearance, appearance for age, gender, cleanliness, style of dress, eye contact, general atti-

tude toward interviewer, and unusual behavior. Appearance and behavior may relate to psychiatric and organic impairment. For example, a slovenly appearance may indicate depression or neglect due to a cerebral vascular (CVA) or substance abuse. Bizarre behavior may indicate acute intoxication, dementia, or a psychotic disorder.

    d. Content and form of thought

        (1) The interviewer should observe to determine that the respondent's speech is logical, goal directed, and coherent. Additionally, content should be free from bizarre ideas or preoccupations suggestive of delusions. Disturbances of thought are often observed with psychotic disorders, dementing disorders, and in cases of acute intoxication.

    e. Language

        (1) The examiner is interested in assessing the respondent's ability to comprehend spoken language as well as his or her ability to express him- or herself effectively. Disturbances in basic language functioning usually indicate organic impairment (e.g., CVA) or acute intoxication.

26. Initial diagnostic impression

    a. The items included on this assessment form have been chosen in order to gather information necessary to diagnose most major categories of psychiatric/substance-use disorders, according to the DSM IV.

27. Initial treatment plan

    a. The identification of problem areas and the rendering of a diagnosis usually serve as the basis of a preliminary treatment plan.

REFERENCES

Addiction Research Foundation. (1993). *Directory of client outcome measures for addictions treatment program.* Toronto: Addiction Research Foundation.

Allen, J. P., & Columbus, M. (Eds.)(1995). *Assessing alcohol problems: A guide for clinicians and researchers.* Bethesda, MD: National Institute on Alcohol Abuse and Alcoholism.

Allen, J. P., & Litten, R. Z. (1993). Psychometric and laboratory measures to assist in the treatment of alcoholism. *Clinical Psychology Review, 13,* 223–239.

Allen, J. P., & Mattson, M. E. (1993). Psychometric instruments to assist in alcoholism treatment planning. *Journal of Substance Abuse Treatment, 10,* 289–296.

American Psychiatric Association. (1994). *Diagnostic and statistical manual of mental disorders* (4th ed.). Washington, DC: Author.

Anastasi, A. (1982). *Psychological testing* (5th ed.). New York: Macmillan.

Annis, H. M. (1986). A relapse prevention model for the treatment of alcoholics. In W. R. Miller & N. Heather (Eds.), *Treating addictive behaviors: Processes of change* (pp. 407–435). New York: Pergamon Press.

Annis, H. M., Graham, J. M., & Davis, C. S. (1987). *Inventory of drinking situations (IDS) user's guide.* Toronto: Addiction Research Foundation.

Annis, H., Martin, G., & Graham, J. M.(1992). *Inventory of drug-taking situations: Users' guide.* Toronto: Addiction Research Foundation.

Babor, T. F., Kranzler, H. R., & Lauerman, R. J. (1989). Early detection of harmful alcohol consumption: Comparison of clinical, laboratory, and self-report screening procedures. *Addictive Behaviors, 14,* 139–157.

Benton, A. L. (1974). *Revised Visual Retention Test: Manual.* New York: Psychological Corporation.

Brown, S. A., Christiansen, B. A., & Goldman, M. S. (1987). The Alcohol Expectancy Questionnaire: An instrument for the assessment of adolescent and adult alcohol expectancies. *Journal of Studies on Alcohol, 48,* 483–491.

Butcher, J. N., Dahlstrom, W. G., Graham, J. R., Tellegen, A., & Daemmer, B. (1989). *MMPI-2 Minnesota Multiphasic Personality Inventory-2: Manual for administration and scoring.* Minneapolis: University of Minnesota Press.

Butcher, J. N., Williams, C. L., Graham, J. R., Archer, R. P., Tellegen, A., Ben-Porath, Y. S., & Kaemmer, B. (1992). *MMPI-A (Minnesota Multiphasic Personality Inventory-Adolescent): Manual for administration, scoring and interpretation.* Minneapolis: University of Minnesota Press.

Connors, G. J. (1995). Screening for alcohol problems. In J. P. Allen & M. Columbus (Eds.), *Assessing alcohol problems: A guide for clinicians and researchers.* Bethesda, MD: National Institute on Alcohol Abuse and Alcoholism.

Council on Scientific Affairs. (1987). Scientific issues in drug testing. *Journal of the American Medical Association, 257*(22), 3110–3114.

Edwards, G., & Gross, M. M. (1976). Alcohol dependence: Provisional description of a clinical syndrome. *British Medical Journal, 1,* 1058–1061.

Ewing, J. A. (1984). Detecting alcoholism. The CAGE questionnaire. *Journal of the American Medical Association, 252*(14), 1905–1907.

Ewing, J. A., & Rouse, B. A. (1970). Indentifying the hidden alcoholic. Presented at the 29th International Congress on Alcohol and Drug Dependence, Sydney, Australia, February 3, 1970.

Fagerstrom, K. O. (1978). Measuring degree of physical dependence to tobacco smoking with reference to individualization of treatment. *Addictive Behaviors, 3,* 235–241.

Fleming, M. F. (1993). Screening and brief intervention for alcohol disorders. *The Journal of Family Practice, 37*(3), 231–234.

Folstein, M. F., Folstein, S. E., & McHugh, P. R. (1975). Mini-Mental State: A practical method for grading the cognitive state of patients for the clinician. *Journal of Psychiatric Research, 12*(3), 189–198.

Gottesman, I. I., & Prescott, C. A. (1989) Abuses of the MacAndrew MMPI Alcoholism Scale: A critical review. *Clinical Psychology Review,* 9, 223–242.

Grant, B. F., & Hasin, D. S. (1991). *The Alcohol Use Disorders and Associated Disabilities Interview Schedule.* Rockville, MD: National Institute on Alcohol Abuse and Alcoholism.

Grant, B. F., & Towle, L. H. (1990). Standardized diagnostic interviews for alcohol research. *Alcohol, Health & Research World, 14,* 340–348.

Grant, I. (1987). Alcohol and the brain: Neuropsychological correlates. *Journal of Consulting and Clinical Psychology, 55*(3), 310–324.

Gripshover, D. L., & Dacey, C. M. (1994). Discriminative validity of the MacAndrew Scale in settings with a high base rate of substance abuse. *Journal of Studies on Alcohol, 55,* 303–308.

Hasin, D. S. (1991). Diagnostic interviews for assessment: Background, reliability, validity. *Alcohol, Health, & Research World, 15*(4), 293–302.

Heatherton, T. F., Kozlowski, L. T., Frecker, R. C., & Fagerstrom, K. O. (1991). The Fagerstrom Test for Nicotine Dependence: A revision of the Fagerstrom Tolerance Questionnaire. *British Journal of Addiction, 86*(7), 1119–1127.

Herman, J. L., Perry, J. C., & van der Kolk, B. A. (1989). Childhood trauma in borderline personality disorder. *American Journal of Psychiatry, 146,* 490–495.

Hien, D., & Levin, F. R. (1994). Trauma and trauma-related disorders for women on methadone: Prevalence and treatment considerations. *Journal of Psychoactive Drugs, 26*(4), 421–429.

Hoeksema, H. L., & deBock, G. H. (1993). The value of laboratory tests for the screening and recognition of alcohol abuse in primary care patients. *The Journal of Family Practice, 37*(3), 268–276.

Johnson, C. A., Pentz, M. A., Weber, M. D., Dwyer, J. H., Baer, N., MacKinnon, D. P., Hansen, W. B., & Flay, B. R. (1990). Relative effectiveness of comprehensive community programming for drug abuse prevention with high-risk and low-risk adolescents. *Journal of Consulting and Clinical Psychology, 58*(4), 447–456.

Johnson, J. L. (1991). Preventive interventions for children at risk: Introduction. *The International Journal of the Addictions, 25*(4A), 429–434.

Kaminer, Y., Bukstein, O., & Tarter, R. E., (1991). The Teen-Addiction Severity Index: Rationale and reliability. *International Journal of Addictions, 26*, 219–226.

Leigh, G., & Skinner, H. A. (1988). Physiological assessment. In D. M. Donovan & G. A. Marlatt (Eds.), *Assessment of addictive behaviors*, (pp. 113–133). New York: The Guilford Press.

Liskow, B., Campbell, J., Nickel, E. J., & Powell, B. J. (1995). Validity of the CAGE questionnaire in screening for alcohol dependence in a walk-in (triage) clinic. *Journal of Studies on Alcohol, 56*, 277–281.

MacAndrew, C. (1965). The differentiation of male alcoholic outpatients from nonalcoholic psychiatric outpatients by means of the MMPI. *Quarterly Journal of Studies on Alcohol, 26*, 238–246.

MacAndrew, C. (1981). What the MAC scale tells us about men alcoholics: An interpretive review. *Journal of Studies on Alcohol, 42*, 604–623.

McLellan, A. T., Luborsky, L., Woody, G. E., & O'Brien, C. P. (1980). An improved diagnostic evaluation instrument for substance abuse patients: The Addiction Severity Index. *The Journal of Nervous and Mental Disease, 168*(1), 26–33.

McLellan, A. T., Kushner, H., Metzger, D., Peters, R., Smith, I., Grissom, G., Pettinati, H., & Argeriou, M. (1992). The fifth edition of the Addiction Severity Index. *Journal of Substance Abuse Treatment, 9*, 199–213.

Mayer, J., & Filstead, W. J. (1979). The Adolescent Alcohol Involvement Scale: An instrument for measuring adolescent use and misuse of alcohol. *Currents in Alcoholism, 7*, 169–181.

Mayfield, D., McLeod, G., & Hall, P. (1974). The CAGE questionnaire: Validation of a new alcoholism screening instrument. *American Journal of Psychiatry, 131*(10), 1121–1123.

Othmer, E., & Othmer, S. C. (1994). *The clinical interview using DSM-IV: Volume 1: Fundamentals.* Washington, DC: American Psychiatric Press.

Parsons, O. A., & Farr, S. P. (1981). The neuropsychology of alcohol and drug use. In S. Filskov & T. J. Boll (Eds.), *Handbook of clinical neuropsychology*, (pp. 320–365). New York: Wiley-Interscience.

Pokorny, A. D., Miller, B. A., & Kaplan, H. B. (1972). The Brief MAST: A shortened version of the Michigan Alcoholism Screening Test. *American Journal of Psychiatry, 129*(3), 342–345.

Pomerleau, C. S., Carton, S. M., Lutzke, M. L., Flessland, K. A., & Pomerleau, O. F. (1994). Reliability of the Fagerstrom Tolerance Questionnaire and the Fagerstrom Test for Nicotine Dependence. *Addictive Behaviors, 19*(1), 33–39.

Reitan, R. (1979). *Trail Making Test for Adults.* Tucson, AZ: Reitan Neuropsychology Laboratory.

Rollnick, S., Heather, N., Gold, R., & Hall, W. (1992). Development of a short readiness to change questionnaire for use in brief, opportunistic interventions among excessive drinkers. *British Journal of Addiction, 87*, 743–754.

Ross, H. E., Gavin, D. R., & Skinner, H. A. (1990). Diagnostic validity of the MAST and the Alcohol Dependence Scale in the assessment of DSM-III alcohol disorders. *Journal of Studies on Alcohol, 51*(6), 506–513.

Salaspuro, M. (1994). Biological state markers of alcohol abuse. *Alcohol Health & Research World, 18*(2), 131–135.

Saunders, J. B., Aasland, O. G., Babor, T. F., De La Fuente, J. R., & Grant, M. (1993). Development of the Alcohol Use Disorders Indentification Test (AUDIT): WHO collaborative project on early detection of persons with harmful alcohol consumption-II. *Addiction, 88*, 791–804.

Schafer, J., & Brown, S. A. (1991). Marijuana and cocaine effect expectancies and drug use patterns. *Journal of Consulting and Clinical Psychology, 59*, 558–565.

Schuckit, M. A. (1995). *Drug and alcohol abuse: A clinical guide to diagnosis and treatment* (4th ed.). New York: Plenum Medical.

Selzer, M. L. (1971). The Michigan Alcoholism Screening Test: The quest for a new diagnostic instrument. *American Journal of Psychiatry, 127*(12), 89–94.

Selzer, M. L., Vinokur, A., & van Rooijen, L. (1975). A self-administered Short Michigan Alcoholism Screening Test (SMAST). *Journal of Studies on Alcohol, 36*, 117–126.

Skinner, H. A. (1982). The Drug Abuse Screening Test. *Addictive Behaviors, 7*, 363–371.

Sobell, L. C., Toneatto, T., & Sobell, M. B. (1994). Behavioral assessment and treatment planning for alcohol, tobacco, and other drug problems: Current status with an emphasis on clinical applications. *Behavior Therapy, 25*(4), 533–580.

Staley, D., & El-Guebaly, N. (1990). Psychometric porperties of the Drug Abuse Screening Test in a psychiatric patient population. *Addictive Behaviors, 15*, 257–264.

Strub, R. L., & Black, F. W. (1985). *The mental status examination in neurology.* (2nd ed.). Philadelphia: F. A. Davis.

Sullivan, J. T., Sykora, K., Schneiderman, J., Naranjo, C. A., & Sellers, E. M. (1989). Assessment of alcohol withdrawal: The Revised Clinical Institute Withdrawal Assessment for Alcohol Scale (CIWA-Ar). *British Journal of Addiction, 84*, 1353–1357.

Tarter, R. E. (1990). Evaluation and treatment of adolescent substance abuse: A decision tree method. *American Journal of Drug and Alcohol Abuse, 16*(1 and 2), 1–46.

Tarter, R. E., & Hegedus, A. M. (1991). The Drug Use Screening Inventory. *Alcohol, Health & Research World, 15*, 65–75.

Triffleman, E. G., Marmar, C. R., Delucchi, K. L., & Ronfeldt, H. (1995). Childhood trauma and posttraumatic stress disorder in substance abuse inpatients. *The Journal of Nervous and Mental Disease, 183*(3), 172–175.

Washton, A. M. (1995). Clinical assessment of psychoactive substance abuse. In A. M. Washton (Ed.), *Psychotherapy and substance abuse: A practitioner's handbook.* New York: Guilford Press.

Wasyliw, O. R., Haywood, T. W., Grossman, L. S., & Cavanaugh, J. L. (1993). The psychometric assessment of alcoholism in forensic groups: The MacAndrew Scale and response bias. *Journal of Personality Assessment, 60*(2), 252–266.

Watson, C. G., Detra, E., Fox, K. L., Ewing, J. W., Gearhart, L. P., & Demotts, J. R. (1995). Comparative concurrent validities of five alcoholism measures in a psychiatric hospital. *Journal of Clinical Psychology, 51*(5), 676–684.

Wechsler, D. (1981). *Wechsler Adult Intelligence Scale-Revised.* New York: Harcourt Brace Jovanovich.

Weed, N. C., Butcher, J. N., & Williams, C. L. (1994). Development of MMPI-A alcohol/drug problem scales. *Journal of Studies on Alcohol, 55*, 296–302.

White, H. R., & Labouvie, E. W. (1989). Towards the assessment of adolescent problem drinking. *Journal of Studies on Alcohol, 50*(1), 30–37.

Zaslav, M. R. (1994). Psychology of comorbid posttraumatic stress disorder and substance abuse: Lessons from combat veterans. *Journal of Psychoactive Drugs, 26*(4), 393–400.

7

DIAGNOSIS AND COMORBIDITY

DEFINITION AND PREVALENCE

Comorbidity exists when a person suffers from more than one disease (Sheehan, 1993). Specifically, in the area of substance abuse, the term refers to the coexistence of a psychoactive substance use disorder and a psychological disorder, each defined by DSM IV (American Psychiatric Association, 1994) diagnostic criteria. The terms *dually diagnosed, dually impaired*, and *MICA* (mentally impaired chemical abuser) are often used to identify patients who exhibit comorbidity. These are not diagnostic categories recognized in the DSM IV (APA, 1994); rather, these descriptive terms appear in the literature and the language of researchers and clinicians.

Dually impaired patients are of growing concern to clinicians because they represent a large proportion of patients presenting for substance abuse and mental health services (Regier *et al.*, 1990). In addition, the dually impaired patient poses significant diagnostic and treatment difficulties (Schwartz *et al.*, 1993; Sheehan, 1993; Stowell, 1991), which often contribute to disappointing treatment outcomes (Corty, Lehman, & Meyers, 1993; Gorski, 1994; Nuckols & Repotosky, 1994). An extensive and widely cited study, the Epidemiological Catchment Area (ECA) Study (Regier *et al.*, 1990), found that nearly 65% of those presenting for drug abuse treatment exhibited psychiatric comorbidity. Conversely, Miller, Belkin, and Gibbons (1994) reported that rates of substance abuse for those presenting for mental health treatment have been found to vary between 25% and 75%, with an average of about 50%. The ECA study is a National Institute of Mental Health (NIMH)–sponsored survey, which employed an extremely large pool of more than 20,000 subjects. A further examination of the results of the ECA study is presented next.

Percentage of Alcohol Abusers Presenting with Comorbid Psychiatric Disorders

1. Anxiety disorders in 19.4% of the cases
2. Antisocial personality disorder in 14.3% of the cases
3. Mood disorder in 13.4% of the cases
4. Schizophrenia in 3.8% of the cases

Percentage of Drug Abusers Presenting with Comorbid Psychiatric Disorders

1. Anxiety disorders in 28.3% of the cases
2. Affective disorders in 26.4% of the cases
3. Antisocial personality disorder in 17.8% of the cases
4. Schizophrenia in 6.8% of the cases

Percentage of Psychiatric Cases Presenting with Substance Abuse or Dependence

1. People with antisocial personality disorder also suffered from substance abuse or dependence in 83.6% of the cases.
2. Forty-seven percent of schizophrenics met the criteria for substance abuse or dependence.
3. People with mood disorders also experienced substance abuse disorders in 32% of the cases.
4. Those with anxiety disorders met the criteria for a substance abuse disorder 24% of the time.

DIAGNOSTIC ISSUES OF THE DUALLY IMPAIRED

Complicating Factors

Clearly, from a treatment perspective, comorbidity is a significant problem; the dually impaired are not very successful in treatment (Corty *et al.*, 1993; Greenfield, Weiss, & Tohen, 1995). As Corty and colleagues (1993) have pointed out, the dually impaired show higher rates of hospitalization and suicidal behavior and are more likely to terminate treatment prematurely. The poor response to treatment is attributable in part to diagnostic problems (Anthenelli, 1994; Chappel, 1995; Dodgen & Kadish, 1992; Gorski, 1994; Greenfield *et al.*, 1995; McKenna & Ross, 1994; Milling, Faulkner, & Craig, 1994) and, consequently, misguided treatment. An additional complication is the problems posed by the coexistence of disorders, each of which may influence the clinical presentation and course of the other (Sheehan, 1993).

Substance abusers with dual diagnoses present serious diagnostic challenges to clinicians in this field. First, substance abuse can cause or exacerbate symptoms characteristic of any psychological condition (Chappel, 1995; Dodgen & Kadish, 1992; Gorski, 1994). For example, amphetamine intoxication can present as psychosis (Corty *et al.*, 1993) and alcohol intoxication can induce antisocial behavior. Also, withdrawal symptoms often appear as psychiatric symptoms. For example, the dysphoria experienced from cocaine withdrawal (Corty *et al.*, 1993) can give the appearance of depression. Prolonged abstinence syndromes can last for months. In addition to the physiologically based dysphoria associated with withdrawal from many substances, by the time someone with a substance abuse problem presents for treatment, serious consequences have been experienced in one or more major realms of functioning: social, marital, familial, vocational, financial, legal, moral–spiritual, emotional, and physical. The experience of negative consequences undoubtedly leads to emotional distress. The question facing the evaluating clinician is whether the observed and reported symptoms are secondary to substance abuse or an indication of a comorbid psychological disorder (Dodgen & Kadish, 1992). Further complicating the diagnostic picture, substances can also mask psychiatric symptoms. For example, opioids can suppress psychotic symptoms and alcohol can mask anxiety symptoms.

Another diagnostic problem of the dually impaired occurs because of denial–minimization of the substance abuse when they report symptoms (Anthenelli, 1994; Dodgen & Kadish, 1992; Milling *et al.*, 1994). In addition to intentional under-reporting of substance abuse, poor histories can also reflect impaired memory due to organicity or mental disorganization (Anthenelli, 1994; Milling *et al.*, 1994). When substance abuse is not reported to an evaluating clinician, symptoms created or worsened by ongoing substance abuse are attributed solely to behavioral, cognitive, or emotional dysfunction (Dodgen & Kadish, 1992). An obvious hazard of such a situation as the one just described is the overestimation of the severity of psychiatric disturbance and the neglect of a substance abuse problem, and subsequent treatment errors. Of equal concern is the masking of psychiatric symptoms by unreported substance abuse. In this latter instance, an existing disorder would be missed because the symptoms are hidden from the evaluating clinician. Finally, the clinical picture can vary significantly depending on whether the person is experiencing withdrawal or intoxication at the time of assessment.

Adding to diagnostic difficulties is the fact that traditional screening and assessment instruments for substance abuse and psychological disorders have not been validated for comorbid populations (Corty *et al.*, 1993; Ross, 1995).

Finally, contributing to the misdiagnosis of the dually impaired is the continued existence of two separate treatment systems for substance-abuse and mental health services, each with different philosophies. Professionals within each field may not have sufficient training in the assessment and treatment of disorders beyond their specific expertise (Chappel, 1995; Sheehan, 1993; Shulman, 1995; Ziedonis & Fisher, 1994). Mental health professionals traditionally either failed to recognize and diagnose substance use disorders, or they considered the symptoms secondary to mental illness with the assumption that substance abuse would spontaneously remit with effective treatment of the mental illness. On the other hand, substance abuse counselors have historically exhibited the opposite bias. They viewed psychiatric symptoms as secondary to substance abuse. Therefore, mental health interventions were not considered necessary.

Treating one or the other condition as primary is obviously simplistic. Indeed, Meyer (1986) described six possible relationships between comorbid psychiatric and substance abuse disorders:

1. Psychiatric symptoms are secondary to substance abuse.
2. A psychiatric condition can alter the course and presentation of substance abuse symptoms.
3. Substance abuse symptoms are secondary to psychiatric dysfunction.
4. A substance abuse condition alters the course and presentation of the psychiatric condition.
5. Substance abuse and psychiatric conditions are the result of a common vulnerability.
6. Substance abuse and psychiatric conditions are independent, but they just happen to present simultaneously.

Improvement of Diagnostic Validity

There are multiple ways to improve diagnostic validity with the dually impaired. Regarding the problem of substance abuse causing or exacerbating psychiatric symptoms, several procedures can be employed to assist in the differential diagnostic process: performance of a thorough psychosocial history (Dodgen & Kadish, 1992), observation of the patient's response to treatment (Dodgen & Kadish, 1992; McKenna & Ross, 1994), and awareness of high-risk factors (McKenna & Ross, 1994) are discussed next.

The completion of a psychosocial history is important when attempting to establish the order of emergence of substance abuse and psychiatric symptoms. With histories evidencing psychiatric disturbance that clearly predated any substance abuse, the problems currently observed and reported would not likely be significantly improved solely by the cessation of substance abuse. Conversely, a fairly typical history is that of someone with a substance abuse syndrome reporting psychiatric symptoms after the start of substance abuse, especially when experiencing withdrawal from the substance or after the experience of significant negative consequences. In this latter scenario, the distress experienced is most likely a secondary effect of substance abuse and would therefore remit with abstinence. The inclusion of collaterals in history-taking is recommended, given the difficulties of the dually impaired to report accurate histories (Milling *et al.*, 1994).

It is important when gathering history to specifically inquire about periods of abstinence of at least 2 to 3 months (Anthenelli, 1994). If, during these extended periods of abstinence, psychiatric symptoms are not present, then they are probably secondary symptoms. If, however, psychiatric symptoms endure during lengthy periods of abstinence, they require specific attention in the treatment.

Observation of a person's response to treatment aids the diagnostic process. Typically, within approximately 4 weeks after complete detoxification and the establishment of abstinence, psychiatric symptoms remit in most patients in the absence of pressing crises (Anthenelli, 1994; Brown, 1995; Dodgen & Kadish, 1992; McKenna & Ross, 1994). Symptoms that persist beyond the 4-week time period give rise to the concern that they are not simply secondary phenomena of substance abuse but indicators of primary psychiatric disturbance.

Finally, knowledge of high-risk groups alerts clinicians to the possibility of dual impairment; awareness of high-risk groups can provide an evaluating clinician with an edge. A patient exhibiting specific risk characteristics would raise the index of suspicion for possible dual impairment. McKenna & Ross (1994) conducted a study to identify variables related to dual impairment. Four variables significantly associated with dual impairment were as follows:

1. Early sexual abuse (significant at $<.09$)
2. An emotionally motivated rationale for substance abuse (i.e., to reduce tension, nervousness, or anxiety or to reduce emotional pain or uncomfortable feelings) (significant at $<.07$)
3. Use of four substances (significant at $<.05$)
4. Relatively late age of onset compared to substance abuse only; the dually diagnosed group began substance abuse at 23 years of age compared to 18.5 for the substance abuse only group (significant at $<.05$).

Illustrative Clinical Cases

The two cases summarized and presented next illustrate methods that may be employed to assist the clinician in performing a differential diagnosis.

Case 1

Tony is a 21-year-old single male, court-ordered for evaluation. He was arrested for trespassing, public nudity, and assault approximately 1 month prior to evaluation. Tony reported that he and three friends were celebrating the end of the college semester by partying for 3 straight days. Tony used cocaine continuously for 3 days; he did not sleep through the entire binge. On the 3rd day of use, Tony began to experience thoughts that he was a werewolf, that others identified him as such, and that they meant to do him harm. He was running naked through the streets when spotted by the police. In an attempt to escape, he ran into a store; a fight ensued with one of the customers of the store where the police apprehended Tony. Tony violently resisted arrest and the police report indicated that Tony was speaking incoherently and was clearly "out of touch with reality."

Tony reported a history of cocaine use starting at 16 years of age. He uses cocaine, snorting, usually only on the weekends. Prior to the arrest was the only time he used in a binge manner. Tony began using alcohol at age 14, getting intoxicated nearly every weekend. He does not use alcohol much except to help him to sleep after using cocaine. Tony smokes one to two packs of cigarettes per day. He is in college with a B to C average, but he feels he could do better if he tried. Tony reported no previous psychiatric treatment and no prior symptoms like those experienced on the day of his arrest. There was no reported history of family substance abuse or psychiatric treatment. The referral question included concern that Tony may have a severe psychiatric disorder in addition to the more obvious problems of substance abuse.

Tony's mother was included in the evaluation to ensure that an accurate report was provided. Tony did not present with any bizarre or unusual behavior and was completely free of psychotic symptoms since a day or so after his arrest. Tony received treatment in an intensive outpatient substance abuse treatment program in addition to individual psychotherapy. After 3 months of treatment in which he was completely abstinent from all psychoactive substances, he remained free of psychotic symptoms.

Tony's case exemplifies a circumstance where psychiatric symptoms were clearly secondary to substance abuse. As he presented to the police, Tony was psychotic and agitated; however, once abstinent these symptoms quickly remitted and never resurfaced. Supporting the conclusion that the symptoms were secondary to substance abuse was the fact that there was no prior history of psychiatric disturbance; his family history also showed no psychiatric disturbance. No treatment was indicated for the psychiatric symptoms that were observed at the time of Tony's arrest.

Case 2

Donald is a 47-year-old married man. He has been employed as a mechanical engineer at the same company for 17 years. He recently received a DWI (driving while intoxicated), his first, and was mandated to undergo an assessment and treatment, if necessary. He reported the following history of alcohol use. Donald began drinking at age 16; he used on weekends in college, never with any signs of impairment. His use gradually increased with his work responsibility; he entertains clients and often has two to three vodka drinks with lunch (approximately three times per week). He reportedly finds client meetings very stressful and feels the alcohol helps "take the edge off" and makes him more effective in the meetings. Donald has been scared by the DWI and has been abstinent for the 6 weeks since arrested. He has reported the emergence of the following symptoms since abstinent: feels nervous and jittery all the time, is restless, has difficulty falling asleep, and has difficulty concentrating and maintaining mental focus. He remembered feeling this way for as far back as middle school.

In Donald's case there are several clues that he suffers from an alcohol use disorder as well as a separate anxiety disorder. He reported explicit use of alcohol to tranquilize his nerves. Also, upon cessation of the use of alcohol, Donald's anxiety increased beyond the time frame expected due to withdrawal. Finally, the experience of anxiety symptoms predated alcohol use (dating back to middle school). Therefore, in addition to treatment for alcohol abuse, Donald required treatment for the anxiety disorder.

Methods to enhance the clinician's chances of detecting unreported or underreported substance abuse include the following (Anthenelli, 1994; Dodgen & Kadish, 1992; Ziedonis & Fisher, 1994):

1. Use of laboratory testing
2. Inclusion of collaterals in the assessment process
3. Awareness on the part of clinicians of the behaviors associated with substance abuse
4. Review of prior treatment records for substance abuse treatment or involvement of substance abuse in previous mental health treatment

To address the diagnostic problems related to the existence of separate treatment systems for substance abuse and psychiatric problems, cross-training of treatment providers, and integration of services and programs is strongly recommended.

TREATMENT OF THE DUALLY DIAGNOSED

Traditional Approaches

The challenge of treatment for the dually diagnosed is that treatment needs are generally even greater than for the nondually diagnosed. A key question is whether the dually diagnosed patient requires specific or modified treatment. Do traditional psychological or substance abuse treatment approaches adequately address the dually diagnosed patient (Dodgen & Kadish, 1992)? The poor outcomes usually achieved by dually diagnosed patients reflect negatively on traditional treatment approaches (Drake, McLaughlin, Pepper, & Minkoff, 1991). Typically, these patients entered treatment through a self-selection process (Shulman, 1995) in one system or the other. If they started in a mental health system, the psychiatric condition was considered primary and was treated; if they started in a substance abuse treatment program, the substance abuse was considered primary and treated. Sometimes after completion of one form of treatment, the patient was referred to a program–provider in the other system for additional care. This serial approach to treatment of the dually diagnosed patient is widely thought of as inadequate (Drake *et al.*, 1991; Minkoff, 1991; Ries, 1993; Shulman, 1995). The lack of continuity of services and the conflictual treatment philosophies (specifically regarding the use of prescribed medication, the need for abstinence, and the importance of self-help groups and education) provide limited help to these vulnerable patients.

Parallel Treatment Systems

Many authors agree that parallel or, ideally, integrated (hybridized) services represent significant improvements over treatment in one system or serial treatment (Drake *et al.*, 1991; Minkoff, 1991; Ries, 1993). In a parallel system, substance abuse and psychiatric treatments are provided simultaneously but in separate programs. For example, a patient admitted to an inpatient psychiatric unit would also receive services such as Narcotics Anonymous (NA) or Alcoholics Anonymous (AA) and 12-step meetings in a substance abuse unit. An example of parallel treatment on an outpatient basis would be if a client in a substance abuse program would also receive the services of a psychiatrist, if necessary, or a psychotherapist, both of whom may or may not be employed by the substance abuse program. Practical problems exist in the implementation of parallel programs including the coordination of transportation and treatment schedules when providers are in separate locations. Communication between professionals also requires additional time and commitment.

Integrated Treatment Systems

In an integrated model, there is explicit cross-training of professionals who work together. Fundamental concepts underlying an integrated model include the following (Minkoff, 1991):

1. Chronic mental disorders and substance abuse are both chronic mental illnesses.
2. Each illness fits into a disease and recovery model.
3. Each illness is primary.
4. Both illnesses have parallel phases of treatment and recovery.
5. Recovery processes proceed independently, but each affects the progress of the other.

In terms of program development, it is important to consider the diversity of patients with dual diagnoses. For example, the treatment needs of an alcoholic with a dysthymic disorder are significantly different from the needs of an alcoholic with chronic schizophrenia. To develop an individual treatment plan, the levels of disability, personal strengths and weaknesses, and family and community resources must be evaluated. A broad spectrum of services must be available to assist the diverse range of problems of this population.

To intervene effectively with patients with dual diagnoses, alterations of traditional psychotherapeutic and substance abuse treatment programs must be made. In traditional substance abuse programs staffed by recovering addicts, the importance of psychotropic medications in treating psychological disorders may not receive sufficient emphasis. Treatment is primarily group based, and involvement in self-help fellowships is promoted. The substance abuse counselor emphasizes personal responsibility and behavior change is brought about through repeated, direct confrontation (Dodgen & Kadish, 1992; Ries, 1993). Problems applying this approach to patients with coexisting psychological and substance abuse disorders stem from the difficulties of certain psychiatric patients in engaging with and benefiting from such treatments. For example, patients with limited ego strength may be unable to tolerate direct confrontation; depressed patients may suffer from a lack of motivation to attend meetings; more disturbed patients may lack the level of mental organization and interpersonal skills to make constructive use of the treatment.

In contrast to traditional substance abuse programs, mental health treatment usually involves the services of psychiatrists, psychologists, or social workers who work together to provide therapy. Treatment emphasizes identification and verbalization of feelings, thoughts, and historical antecedents to current behavior (Dodgen & Kadish, 1992; Ries, 1993). Therapists typically engage in empathic listening, interpretation, and relationship building in an effort to create more effective coping skills and behavior change. Substance abuse problems may be given relatively little direct attention. This can be a problem because active substance abuse during treatment is a destructive force to psychotherapy on at least two levels: (a) To the extent that the patient is abusing psychoactive substances, functional or organic impairments may interfere with the ability to absorb and integrate new information necessary for behavior change. (b) Impulsive gratification through substance use and repression of feelings may interfere with the goals of therapy.

In an integrated treatment model, clinicians blend the two traditional treatment approaches. With the lower functioning patients, less aggressive confrontation is employed. Also, with this lower functioning group, abstinence would be considered an eventual goal rather than an initial, absolute requirement. There are those who feel that initial abstinence is too rigorous a requirement for many dually diagnosed patients (Carey, 1989; Levy, 1993; Nikkel, 1994). Effective treatment of the dually diagnosed patient centers on assessment and enhancement of motivation along with skill-building (Nikkel, 1994). Skill-based interventions range from the basic recognition and acknowledgment of the devastating role of substance abuse in one's problems, to relapse prevention, to self-care.

Securing adequate housing and development of transportation skills may be necessary for lower functioning patients.

REFERENCES

American Psychiatric Association. (1994). *Diagnostic and statistical manual of mental disorders* (4th ed.). Washington, DC: Author.
Anthenelli, R. M. (1994). The initial evaluation of the dual diagnosis patient. *Psychiatric Annals, 24*(8), 407–411.
Brown, S. A. (1995). Accurate dual diagnosis aided by 'wait and see.' *American Journal of Psychiatry, 152*, 45–52.

Carey, B. K. (1989). Treatment of the mentally ill chemical abuser: Description of the Hutchings Day Treatment Program. *Psychiatric Quarterly, 60*(4), 303–316.

Chappel, J. H. (1995). Dual diagnosis: A psychiatric perspective. *Behavioral Health Management, 15,* 34–36.

Corty, E., Lehman, A. F., & Myers, C. P. (1993). Influence of psychoactive substance use on the reliability of psychiatric diagnosis. *Journal of Consulting and Clinical Psychology, 61*(1), 165–170.

Dodgen, C. E., & Kadish, L. (1992). Critical issues in the treatment of the dually diagnosed patient. *New Jersey Psychologist, 42*(4), 22–25.

Drake, R. E., McLaughlin, P., Pepper, B., & Minkoff, K. (1991). Dual diagnosis of major mental illness and substance disorder: An overview. *New Directions for Mental Health Services, 50,* 3–12.

Gorski, T. T. (1994). A suggestion for conceptualizing dual diagnosis: A systematic analysis to help cut through the confusion and mismanagement. *Behavioral Health Management, 14,* 50–55.

Greenfield, S. F., Weiss, R. D., & Tohen, M. (1995). Substance abuse and the chronically mentally ill: A description of dual diagnosis treatment services in a psychiatric hospital. *Community Mental Health Journal, 31*(3), 265–277.

Levy, M. (1993). Psychotherapy with dual diagnosis patients: Working with denial. *Journal of Substance Abuse Treatment, 10,* 499–504.

McKenna, C., & Ross, C. (1994). Diagnostic conundrums in substance abusers with psychiatric symptoms: Variables suggestive of dual diagnosis. *American Journal of Drug and Alcohol Abuse, 20,* 397–413.

Meyer, R. E. (1986). How to understand the relationship between psychopathology and addictive disorders: Another example of the chicken and the egg. In R. E. Meyer (Ed.), *Psychopathology and addictive disorders* (pp. 3–16). New York: Guilford.

Miller, N. S., Belkin, B. M., & Gibbons, R. (1994). Clinical diagnosis of substance use disorders in private psychiatric populations. *Journal of Substance Abuse Treatment, 11*(4), 387–392.

Milling, R. N., Faulkner, L. R., & Craig, J. M. (1994). Problems in the recognition and treatment of patients with dual diagnoses. *Journal of Substance Abuse Treatment, 11*(3), 267–271.

Minkoff, K. (1991). Program components of a comprehensive integrated care system for serious mentally ill patients with substance disorders. In K. Minkoff & R. E. Drake (Eds.), *Dual diagnosis of major mental illness and substance disorder* (pp. 13–28). San Francisco: Jossey-Bass.

Nikkel, R. E. (1994). Clinical care update: Areas of skill training for persons with mental illness and substance use disorders. Building skills for successful community living. *Community Mental Health Journal, 30*(1), 61–72.

Nuckols, C. C., & Repotosky, J. (1994). Clinical observations on the dually diagnosed. *Behavioral Health Management, 14,* 36–38.

Regier, D. A., Farmer, M. E., Rae, D. S., Locke, B. Z., Keith, S. J., Judd, L. L., & Goodwin, F. K. (1990). Comorbidity of mental disorders with alcohol and other drug abuse: Results from the Epidemiologic Catchment Area (ECA) study. *Journal of the American Medical Association, 264*(19), 2511–2518.

Ries, R. (1993). Clinical treatment matching models for dually diagnosed patients. *Psychiatric Clinics of North America, 16*(1), 167–175.

Ross, H. E. (1995). Popular screening interviews unreliable for dual diagnosis. *Alcohol and Drug Abuse, 7,* 3–4.

Schwartz, L. S., Lyons, J. S., Stulp, F., Hassan, T., Jacobi, N., & Taylor, J. (1993). Assessment of alcoholism among dually diagnosed psychiatric inpatients. *Journal of Substance Abuse Treatment, 10,* 255–261.

Sheehan, M. F. (1993). Dual diagnosis. *Psychiatric Quarterly, 64,* 107–133.

Shulman, G. D. (1995). Reorienting cd treatment for dual diagnosis. *Behavioral Health Management, 15,* 30–34.

Stowell, R. J. (1991). Dual diagnosis issues. *Psychiatric Annals 21*(2), 98–104.

Ziedonis, D. M., & Fisher, W. (1994). Assessment and treatment of comorbid substance abuse in individuals with schizophrenia. *Psychiatric Annals, 24*(9), 477–483.

8

TREATMENT I: MODELS AND APPROACHES

TREATMENT SETTINGS AND SERVICES

Clinicians working in the area of substance abuse are most likely familiar with the settings within which substance abuse treatment is offered. To determine the most appropriate treatment setting, alternatives from a number of dimensions exist (Dodgen, 1994). One choice is professional versus nonprofessional services. Typically, nonprofessional alternatives include Alcoholics Anonymous (AA), Narcotics Anonymous (NA), Cocaine Anonymous (CA), and Double Trouble. These are 12-step programs of recovery for alcoholics, drug abusers, cocaine abusers, and the dually impaired, respectively. Professional treatment options include services of a mental health or substance abuse professional or a formal substance abuse treatment program. Especially in the early phase of treatment and with those individuals who are more severely addicted, individual therapy alone is considered inadequate treatment for substance use disorders (Rawson, 1995). Individual therapies, however, are frequently effective as a part of multicomponent treatment programs.

Treatment choices exist between inpatient- and outpatient-based programs. Inpatient treatment involves residence at the treatment facility. Outpatient treatment, in contrast, refers to a situation in which the patient lives at home and receives services at the treatment facility or professional office. Inpatient treatment is generally more extensive, more intensive, and costlier than outpatient treatment. One form of inpatient treatment is the traditional rehabilitation program, which typically lasts for 28 days (i.e., the Minnesota Model) within an acute care hospital setting or psychiatric facility. Other types of inpatient treatment programs include halfway and three-quarter houses as well as therapeutic communities. Halfway and three-quarter houses usually function as transitional programs—that is, halfway houses are "half way" between inpatient rehabilitation and community living, offering more structure than living at home but fewer restrictions than the typical rehabilitation program. Three-quarter houses are usually less structured and less restrictive than halfway houses and represent another step toward independent living in the community. Whereas halfway houses maintain formal programming, curfews, meeting requirements, and house responsibilities, three-quarter houses are usually made up of recovering addicts living together who seek their own treatment. Therapeutic communities (TCs) are considered long-term programs and often are 9 to 12 months in duration (see discussion of TCs presented later in this chapter).

In the current treatment climate, inpatient rehabilitation is considered the treatment of last resort. In response to diminishing third-party reimbursement for inpatient treatment, more intensive outpatient alternatives have been developed. Partial hospital programs (PHPs) for substance abusers and intensive outpatient programs are becoming increasingly available.

Placement Criteria

Clinicians must weigh various factors to determine the optimal treatment setting. Needless to say, many different algorithms exist to assist in the placement of substance abuse patients. In an attempt to establish uniform criteria for determining the most appropriate treatment settings for patients, the American Society of Addiction Medicine (ASAM) (1991) published placement standards. The ASAM (1991) criteria were developed for adults and adolescents with psychoactive substance use disorders; placement is based on clinical as well as financial considerations. Individuals can be placed along a continuum of four levels of care, which differ with respect to the following three dimensions: provision of medical management; structure, safety, and security; and intensity of services. The four levels of care are presented as follows:

Level 1. Outpatient treatment. Nonresidential treatment provided in an office practice or other professional setting offering services for fewer than 9 contact hours per week.

Level 2. Intensive outpatient/partial hospital treatment. Nonresidential treatment provided in a professional setting offering services for 9 to 20 contact hours per week.

Level 3. Medically monitored intensive inpatient treatment. Residential program provided in a free-standing licensed health care facility or specialized unit in a general or psychiatric hospital offering 24-hr professionally directed care.

Level 4. Medically managed intensive inpatient treatment. Residential program provided in an acute care general hospital, psychiatric unit in an acute care general hospital, acute psychiatric hospital, or appropriately licensed chemical dependency specialty hospital with acute medical and nursing staff and life support equipment. Services include 24-hr medically directed care requiring primary medical and nursing care.

Placement decisions are based on a thorough assessment of the following six problem areas (ASAM, 1991):

1. Acute intoxication or withdrawal potential
2. Biomedical conditions or complications
3. Emotional/behavioral conditions or complications
4. Treatment acceptance
5. Relapse potential
6. Recovery environment

The goal of the clinician is to place the patient in the least intensive level of care that will facilitate the achievement of treatment goals. As identified problems improve or worsen, placement decisions can be reevaluated.

Some authors (e.g., Book *et al.*, 1995) have criticized the ASAM criteria and developed other placement criteria. Book and colleagues (1995) compared the ASAM (1991) placement criteria to those of Green Spring Health Services, a national managed care program. Book and associates (1995) contend that utilization of ASAM criteria results in an overutilization of inpatient treatment, an overemphasis on the provision of services at the beginning of treatment, and insufficient emphasis on the continuum of care necessary as the patient progresses through recovery. They (Book *et al.*, 1995) have proposed a reduction in the reliance on costly inpatient care by adding levels of outpatient care (e.g., halfway houses and the separation of partial hospitalization and intensive outpatient programs), provision of outpatient detoxification unless contraindicated, and consideration of the concepts of mental competence and restorative potential. That is, if someone cannot benefit from the treatment, they should not receive it (because they would be, essentially, wasting a resource someone else might benefit from). Of course, questions exist about how mental competence and restorative potential can best be determined. By Green Spring standards, inpatient treatment should only be used as a last resort and under specific conditions such as if the patient's life is in danger, serious medical complications exist, or other forms of treatment have failed.

MAJOR THEORETICAL TREATMENT APPROACHES

Treatment implications of various models will be summarized next. They include the psychoanalytic, family therapy, behavioral/cognitive behavioral, motivational interviewing, biopsychosocial, 12-step, and the therapeutic community approaches.

Reviews of psychoanalytic, family, behavioral/ cognitive behavioral, and motivational interviewing (client-centered) approaches to the treatment of substance abuse can be found, respectively, in chapters by Leeds and Morgenstern (1996), McCrady and Epstein (1996), Rotgers (1996), and Bell and Rollnick (1996). A brief summary of the contributions of these authors is presented here.

Current Psychoanalytic/Psychodynamic Approaches

Leeds and Morgenstern (1996; Morgenstern & Leeds, 1993) provide an excellent review and discussion of contemporary psychoanalytic approaches to the understanding and treatment of substance abuse. They (Leeds & Morgenstern, 1996) identified several reasons for the historical neglect of psychoanalytic approaches in the area of substance abuse. Traditionally, substance abuse was considered a secondary, surface manifestation of deeper problems and, therefore, not a focus of direct attention. In addition, psychoanalytic techniques were considered inadequate for substance abusers who were thought to have insufficient ego and intense acting-out defenses. Finally, substance abusers were historically from lower socioeconomic strata and unlikely to present for psychoanalytic treatment.

Leeds and Morgenstern (1996) have identified four contemporary views based on ego psychology and object relations theory that address the question of etiology and of optimum treatment of substance abuse disorders (Khantzian, 1990; Krystal, 1979; McDougal, 1978; Wurmser, 1981).

Neurotic Conflict

Wurmser (1981) viewed neurotic conflict and the presence of a harsh and punitive superego to be at the heart of substance abuse; substances are sought to provide temporary relief from the tyranny of the superego and associated emotional discomfort. Wurmser proposed traditional psychoanalytic treatment as part of a comprehensive program of care involving self-help, pharmacotherapy, education, and family treatment.

Ego- and Self-Deficits

Khantzian (1985) conceptualized substance abuse disorders as stemming from ego- and self-deficits; substance abuse represents an attempt by the abuser to bolster a weak sense of self and compensate for deficient ego functioning, especially in the areas of affect tolerance and object relations. Khantzian's is the only theory that specifically addresses drug of choice, which, in his view, is related to the particular feelings the addict is unable to tolerate or manage. For example, a person might choose opioids to quell rage and anger, a depressed person might abuse stimulants to increase energy and eliminate apathy, and an anxious person might choose alcohol and sedatives to tranquilize anxiety. Khantzian has developed a group-based treatment, Modified Dynamic Group Therapy (Khantzian, 1990) for the treatment of substance abuse. The goals are to help a patient achieve insight and enhance ego functioning; self-help and relapse prevention are also considered important components of this treatment.

Deficits in Affective Functioning and Object Relations

Krystal (1979) regarded substance abuse as the result of primary deficits in affective functioning and object relations. He posited that substance abusers are alexithymic—that is, they are unable to identify basic feeling states and, therefore, exist in an undifferentiated, uncomfortable emotional state most of the time. Regarding disturbance of object relations, borderline pathology with attendant idealization and devaluation of objects is seen as lying at the core of the problem. The abuse of substances is seen as a form of symbolic introjection and merger, with separation and pain experienced during withdrawal from the substance. Krystal has recommended programmatic treatment in which the transference is diluted among several different therapists.

Psychosomatic Disorders

McDougal (1978) viewed substance abuse as similar to psychosomatic disorders; both represent a defense against distress. Internal defensive structures are lacking so that feelings are externalized and discharged in action. Substances are used to reduce pain and awareness of feelings.

Elements Common to Psychoanalytic Theories of Substance Abuse

Although there are differences among these theoretical views, the following common elements emerge (Leeds & Morgenstern, 1996; Morgenstern & Leeds, 1993):

1. Substance abuse is seen as a symptom of more basic disturbance.
2. Problems in the regulation of affect and pathological object relations are core difficulties.

Strengths and Weaknesses of Psychoanalytic Theories of Substance Abuse

Leeds and Morgenstern (1996) viewed the strength of psychoanalytic theories as their consideration of the entire personality rather than treating substance abuse as a problem separate from the rest of the personality of the abuser. They identified the following weaknesses in psychoanalytic theories of substance abuse:

1. They focus on psychogenic factors and the relative neglect of other factors known to contribute to substance abuse (e.g., social, genetic, and pharmacological factors).
2. They make no attempt to discern preexisting problems from those resulting from substance abuse.
3. They view substance abuse disorders as homogeneous.

Family Therapies

McCrady and Epstein (1996) provided an excellent historical review of the evolution of family treatment models of substance abuse. McCrady and Epstein (1996) identified three currently popular models on which most family treatment of substance abuse is based: the family disease, behavioral, and family systems models.

Family Disease Model

The family disease model views substance abuse as a family disease, with the substance abuser preoccupied with substances, and certain family members preoccupied with the abuser (i.e., codependent). Codependent family members can be identified by certain characteristic traits including, but not limited to, low self-esteem, dependency, a tendency to minimize personal needs and put other's needs first, and difficulty with intimacy. Additional characteristics include constriction of emotion, anxiety, depression, hypervigilance, and enmeshment with the substance abuser.

Behavioral Model

The behavioral model of family therapy focuses on patterns of interaction. Behavior patterns appear to be different when alcohol is used. Both abusers and family members may prefer the behavior of the abuser when he or she is intoxicated and therefore reinforce the abuse of substances. For example, an alcohol abuser may be more outgoing and light hearted when drinking and provide family members with a sense of relief and pleasure.

Family Systems Model

The family systems model addresses, primarily, the roles of family members, the boundaries of relationships, rules of conduct, and the maintenance of familial homeostasis. Accordingly, the abuser may resist a change of role (from abuser to nonabuser), and family members may resist the change as well.

Strengths and Weaknesses of Family Theories of Substance Abuse

McCrady and Epstein (1996) have identified the following advantages of family-based approaches:

1. The focus is on factors beyond the individual that may be maintaining substance abuse.
2. The possibility that family involvement in treatment can improve treatment compliance is considered.
3. The involvement of family members can help alleviate their distress related to the substance abuse problem.
4. Research provides a solid empirical basis for treatment.

Disadvantages of family-based treatment include the following (McCrady & Epstein, 1996):

1. The complexity and difficulty of working with many people
2. The difficulty working with families with multiple substance abusers or severe psychopathology
3. The relative neglect of the individual needs of family members

Behavioral/Cognitive Behavioral Approaches

In his excellent chapter, Rotgers (1996) reviewed the basis of behavioral therapies, which includes principles of learning derived from classical conditioning, operant conditioning, and social learning theory.

Classical Conditioning

. Classical conditioning is thought to account for the experience of urges and cravings in response to certain environmental cues. That is, environmental cues become associated, through repeated pairings, with the use of a substance; these cues therefore elicit physiological responses that are experienced as urges for the substance of abuse. Four types of treatment procedures are based on classical conditioning: cue exposure (i.e., extinction), stimulus control techniques, relaxation training, and covert sensitization, discussed further later in this chapter.

Operant Conditioning

The principles of operant conditioning relate to the reinforcing qualities of substance abuse. Substances either produce a positive effect or eliminate negative experience, thereby increasing the likelihood of further use of the substance. A key factor in this process is that reinforcers proximate in time to a certain behavior will have a greater influence on the behavior than those more distal. Therefore, immediate relief brought about through the use of substances is stronger than the pain of more distal negative consequences. Operant learning principles are employed by the Community Reinforcement Approach (discussed in more detail later) in order to enhance treatment compliance.

Social Learning Theory

Social learning theory addresses processes such as modeling; the concept of self-efficacy is a central feature of this theory. Regarding substance abuse, association with peers and family members who model substance use is a well-known risk factor. Treatment procedures based on social learning theory include social skills training, refusal skills, anger management, relaxation, and coping self-statements.

The cognitive mediation of behavior is another important aspect of social learning theory. Thoughts, feelings, and expectations also contribute to behavior. Marlatt and Gordon's (1985) relapse prevention model (discussed later) provides a good example of a cognitive–behavioral treatment approach.

In his summary of behavioral and cognitive-behavioral approaches to the treatment of substance abuse, Rotgers (1996) noted that they do not necessarily require total abstinence for alcohol abusers. Reduction of use and harm-reduction are appropriate, more attainable treatment goals in many cases.

Strengths and Weakness of Behavioral Approaches to the Treatment of Substance Abuse

Rotgers (1996) identified the following advantages of behavioral approaches:

1. Empowerment of clients

2. Improved compliance due to client collaboration in the treatment
3. Flexibility and individualization of treatment

Rotgers (1996) also cited weaknesses of the behavioral approaches, including the following:

1. Possible therapist rejection due to a preference for traditional psychotherapy
2. The lack of emphasis on spirituality
3. The lack of empirical support of effective, long-lasting change through behavioral therapies

Client-Centered/Motivational Interviewing

Client-centered treatment, also known as motivational interviewing, is an approach that stands in stark contrast to traditional substance abuse treatment (Bell & Rollnick, 1996). Instead of relying on aggressive confrontation and direct persuasion, this approach stems from a desire to work with the client at his or her own level of motivation. The style of the therapist is crucial to engaging the client in treatment. Rather than viewing a client as resistant and in denial, the therapist attempts to identify, guide, and magnify the client's motivation to change. The client's level of motivation to change is conceptualized in the model described by Prochaska and DiClemente (1986) (discussed in Chapter 4). Stage of change can be assessed via several instruments, two of which are the SOCRATES (*S*tages *O*f *C*hange *R*eadiness *A*nd *T*reatment *E*agerness *S*cale) (Miller & Tonigan, 1996) and URICA (*U*niversity of *R*hode *I*sland *C*hange *A*ssessment Scale) (discussed in Carney & Kivlahan, 1995). Interventions vary depending on the identified stage of change (Bell & Rollnick, 1996). With precontemplators, who have no internal motivation for treatment, interventions aim to create ambivalence by introducing information about the risks and negative consequences of their substance use. Contemplators, already ambivalent, are engaged in discussion about their substance use, with an emphasis on the negative consequences. Those in the preparation phase need guidance and support for a plan of action. Those in the action stage benefit from positive reinforcement for their behavioral changes. In the maintenance stage, clients may benefit from relapse prevention strategies.

Because in the client-centered approach the client is integrally involved with the treatment process, this method is considered effective in reducing attrition and maintaining compliance with therapeutic goals.

Biopsychosocial Model

The biopsychosocial model is a comprehensive model with which researchers attempt to integrate all known variables thought to contribute to the development and maintenance of psychoactive substance use disorders (Galizio & Maisto, 1985). Proponents of this model (e.g., Galizio & Maisto, 1985) posit that unidimensional models are necessarily inadequate because they fail to account for other factors known to bear some relation to substance abuse. The biopsychosocial model explicitly acknowledges and accepts that biological (genetic predisposition), psychological (e.g., psychodynamics, learning aspects), and social factors (availability, culture, peer and family modeling) must be considered in the etiology and treatment of substance abuse. Although no specific treatment interventions are derived from this model, programs offering comprehensive services are consistent with this approach.

12-Step Programs

Twelve-step programs such as Alcoholics Anonymous (AA) and Narcotics Anonymous (NA) stem from the basic assumption that alcohol or drug abuse are chronic diseases. Therefore, an abuser is never thought of as cured. The 12 steps (Alcoholics Anonymous, 1952) represent a pathway through which an alcoholic can progress in order to restore life to stable sobriety and sanity. Twelve-step programs are the quintessence of self-help programs; they are fellowships of people who suffer with similar problems and rely on one another for help. Recovery is achieved through adherence to the principles, reciprocal support and guidance, and spirituality. AA and NA groups rely on confrontation to crack denial, overpower the cunning disease of addiction, and promote honesty and self-responsibility. Although once thought of as an alternative to traditional psychotherapeutic approaches, 12-step programs are now considered a valuable part of a comprehensive treatment program of primary care or aftercare (Montgomery, Miller, & Tonigan, 1995).

Therapeutic Community

Therapeutic communities (TCs) are long-term, self-help-based, residential programs typically of 9 to 12 months duration (Wexler, 1995). Staff members are usually recovering addicts. TCs are based on the assumption that addicts are immature. Programs are rigidly structured to promote independence, responsibility, and stable relationships. A strong focus is placed on the here and now with residents sharing in all aspects of program development, maintenance of the grounds, and administration of programs (Carroll, 1992; Wexler, 1995). TCs are the boot camp of recovery programs. They provide a hierarchical organization, and residents earn privileges based on their quality of participation in the program. The programs tend to be highly confrontation oriented. In the past, TCs functioned as completely closed systems. Carroll (1992) noted that TCs now recognize the need to collaborate with other programs and professionals to meet the increasingly diverse medical and psychological needs of their residents.

ADDITIONAL PSYCHOLOGICAL THERAPIES

In addition to the treatment procedures based on the previously discussed major theoretical models, specific psychological therapies are frequently used in the treatment of substance abuse. These methods include social skills training, contingency management, aversion therapies, the community reinforcement approach (CRA), relapse prevention, cue exposure, behavioral self-control, stress management, and network therapy.

Social Skills Training

Social skills training is an umbrella term for various interventions such as assertiveness training, anger control, relaxation training, anxiety control, modeling, role playing, behavioral rehearsal, coaching instruction, and feedback (Platt & Husband, 1993). The choice of interventions depends on those skills that are identified as deficient during the assessment phase of treatment. Deficient skills are thought to lead to poor adjustment and dysfunction, contributing to a reliance on substances. Also, deficient social skills appear to place an individual at elevated risk of relapse. The experience of negative affective states associated with social failure and an inability to effectively cope with high-risk situations contribute to possible treatment failures (Platt & Husband, 1993).

Platt and Husband (1993) noted that social skills training is widely used as an adjunct to comprehensive treatment programs. This training is particularly effective in relapse prevention and primary prevention. Some limitations of social skills interventions include a lack of maintenance and poor generalization of skills. Furthermore, the efficacy of social skills training as a stand-alone treatment for substance abuse has not been clearly demonstrated (Platt & Husband, 1993).

Contingency Management

Contingency management is based on operant learning principles. Simply, contingency management is a procedure of encouraging certain desired behaviors by positive reinforcement and discouraging undesirable behavior by removing positive reinforcement. Kadden and Mauriello (1991) demonstrated the ability of this approach to enhance patient compliance in an inpatient substance abuse treatment program. Patients in their study were granted access to desired activities for performing target behaviors such as attending and participating in group therapies and complying with program rules. They found that rewarding target behaviors significantly improved patient compliance.

The community reinforcement approach (CRA) (discussed later) also employs operant conditioning principles.

Aversion Therapies

Two common forms of aversive therapy for substance abusers are covert sensitization and, specifically for alcohol abusers, the use of the pharmacological agent, disulfiram (Antabuse) (discussed in detail later). Covert sensitization is a cognitive–behavioral technique in which personally unpleasant images are incorporated into thoughts and fantasies of substance use. For example, when thinking of using alcohol, the patient might train him- or herself to also imagine losing his or her spouse and job; the originally pleasant expected outcome of use is altered by these negative associations. Covert sensitization is used primarily to interfere with cravings or urges for substance use.

Community Reinforcement Approach (CRA)

The community reinforcement approach (CRA) is not a unidimensional approach but rather a multicomponent approach combining the following treatment elements: marital–family counseling, relapse prevention, employment counseling, and social–recreational counseling (discussed in Miller, 1992, and Rawson, 1995). The goal of the CRA is to make the abuser's life more rewarding (by improving marital–family life, social life, and vocational functioning) so that a natural barrier to relapse is erected. Because relapse would result in the loss of the more gratifying lifestyle, the resumption of abuse is deterred. In addition, operant conditioning principles enhance program participation and compliance by rewarding desired behavior; this aspect of the program (reward system) is very effective in the treatment of both alcohol (Azrin, Sisson, Meyers, & Godley, 1982) and cocaine abuse (Higgins *et al.*, 1994; also see Higgins *et al.*, 1993). For example, Higgins and colleagues (1994) rewarded patients with gift vouchers for producing negative urines throughout the course of treatment. The researchers found that the patients receiving incentives achieved more positive outcomes than those receiving only CRA treatment.

Relapse Prevention

The Marlatt and Gordon (1985) model is the prototype on which most relapse prevention programs are based (Rawson, Obert, McCann, & Martinelli-Casey, 1993a, 1993b). The model is rooted in the principles of social learning theory. Addictive behavior is seen as learned or habitual behavior that can be altered by changing factors known to affect behavior, such as antecedent conditions, beliefs and expectations, and consequences. Marlatt and Gordon (1985) noted that in treatment, too often much emphasis is placed on the initial achievement of abstinence, and not enough attention is placed on maintenance of behavior change. Maintenance of behavior change (i.e., abstinence) is the focus of relapse prevention.

Marlatt and Gordon (1985) described two levels of interventions:

1. Specific interventions. Specific interventions consist of identification of personal high-risk situations, development of strategies to effectively cope with identified high-risk situations, and modification of cognitive and emotional reactions. The goal of these interventions is to prevent a lapse from becoming a full-blown relapse. According to the model, lapses in abstinence ("slips") are inevitable and should be anticipated. A lapse is seen as a critical "choicepoint" whereby an

individual can either return to abstinence or develop a full-blown relapse in response to the experience of the abstinence violation effect (AVE). The AVE is, essentially, a response in which the individual decides to fully abandon the goal of abstinence because it has been violated. For example, an individual might say, "Since I am no longer abstinent, I might as well go all the way." Marlatt and Gordon (1985) have pointed out that certain cognitive factors are strongly related to relapse: a sense of low self-efficacy in high-risk situations, positive expectations about the use of substances, and specific causal attributions. The following causal attributions associated with a lapse are related to the exhibition of the AVE: internal (originated in self), stable (lapse due to an unchanging trait), and global (other situations will result in a lapse). Other authors (Walton, Castro, & Barrington, 1994) have generally supported the findings of Marlatt and Gordon (1985) regarding the relationship between causal attributions and the AVE.

2. Global interventions. Global interventions stress the development of positive, healthy behaviors to replace behaviors associated with substance abuse and to reinforce nonuse of substances (Marlatt & Gordon, 1985).

Common Elements of Relapse Prevention Programs

Rawson and associates (1993a, 1993b) noted that the following elements are common to most relapse-prevention programs:

1. Psychoeducation
2. Identification of high-risk situations and warning signs of relapse
3. Development of skills to cope with high-risk situations
4. Change in lifestyle to positive behaviors
5. Enhancing self-efficacy
6. Avoidance of the AVE
7. Drug–alcohol monitoring through the use of urine or blood testing

Some relapse prevention programs are substance specific (Rawson *et al.*, 1993a, 1993b): Wallace's model (1989) for crack cocaine, Annis's approach (1986) for alcohol, Roffman and Barnhart's model (1987) for marijuana, and the Carroll, Rounsaville, and Keller (1991) model for cocaine abuse. Substance-specific programs may provide advantages of enhanced credibility and patient retention in treatment (Rawson *et al.*, 1993a, 1993b).

Most relapse prevention programs are considered adjunctive. Some clinicians have developed intensive, comprehensive outpatient relapse prevention programs that can function as stand-alone programs (e.g., Rawson, 1993a, 1993b; Washton, 1989).

It has been noted that some professional resistance to relapse prevention programs exists (Baker, Galea, Lewis, Paolantonio, & Tessier-Woupio, 1989). To admit that lapses are expected may be an objectionable premise for those who adhere to the disease model. These clinicians feel that an expectation of relapse may encourage substance use.

Cue Exposure

Cue exposure is a treatment derived from the Pavlovian conditioning paradigm. Environmental cues become conditioned with (i.e., associated with) the use of a substance and can evoke cravings that contribute to relapse (Laberg, 1990). The craving motivates substance use in order to relieve the discomfort of urging or craving (negative reinforcement). Treatment consists of exposure to cues and re-sponse-prevention (i.e., extinction).

One limitation of cue exposure treatment for alcohol (and other substances) is the difficulty of identifying and presenting all relevant cues; social stimulation and mood contribute to the use of substances but are hard to re-create in treatment (Laberg, 1990). Another obstacle relates to involvement of cognitive factors in cue exposure treatment (Laberg, 1990). That is, efficacy expectations appear to be involved with the positive treatment effects of cue exposure; an individual's confidence in the ability to resist cravings may be more important than extinction of the association between cues and substances. The best cue exposure treatment, therefore, may be to increase coping skills and enhance self-efficacy in addition to standard cue exposure.

Behavioral Self-Control

Behavioral self-control interventions are primarily employed for the treatment of alcohol abuse and are multicomponent, behavior modification strategies. Some discrimination training is usually employed; subjects are trained to accurately estimate their blood alcohol level with the aid of a breath analysis device (e.g., Brown, 1980; Caddy & Lovibond, 1976). Traditional behavioral interventions are often used; subjects are trained to alter drinking behavior (e.g., reduce drink strength or increase time between drinks) and are taught to reward themselves for adherence to a targeted blood alcohol level when drinking alcohol (Brown, 1980; Caddy & Lovibond, 1976).

Stress Management

Stress management includes interventions such as biofeedback, relaxation training, desensitization, exercise, and biofeedback (discussed in Miller, 1992).

Network Therapy

Network therapy is a relatively new approach to the treatment of substance abuse. The clinician explicitly attempts to engage the social network (primarily family and friends) of the abuser to help maintain abstinence (Galanter, 1987). Galanter (1987) described the role of the network in terms of providing for support of the patient's abstinence, reinforcing treatment goals of the program, guarding against slips, and guiding the patient back to treatment if relapse occurs.

ROLE OF PHARMACOTHERAPY

Currently, pharmacological treatments are used mainly for management of detoxification from psychoactive substances (Gold & Miller, 1995; Kleber, 1995; Rao, Ziedonis, & Kosten, 1995). Pharmacotherapies are not meant to be stand-alone treatments; nonpharmacological (i.e., psychosocial) treatments are the treatments of choice for substance abuse (Gold & Miller, 1995). The primary goal of pharmacotherapy is to assist the patient in remaining abstinent during acute withdrawal in order to allow other therapies an opportunity to work; facilitation of abstinence during subacute withdrawal (within the first 6 months of treatment) is an unrealized goal. The other effective use of pharmacological agents is in the treatment of comorbid psychiatric disorders (Gold & Miller, 1995).

Pharmacological products that have received the most attention in the literature are aimed at cocaine, alcohol, opioids, and nicotine. Those pharmacological products that have been investigated are discussed next. It should be restated that no pharmacological products have proven to be clearly effective beyond the management of acute withdrawal (i.e., they are all still considered experimental beyond the detoxification phase of treatment).

Cocaine

The course of cocaine withdrawal has been well studied. There appear to be three phases (Kleber, 1995):

1. The crash. This phase lasts from 24 hr to 7 days following cessation of use of cocaine and is characterized by intense dysphoria, depressed mood, suicidal ideation, agitation, craving for cocaine, and fatigue.
2. Withdrawal phase. This phase lasts from 2 to 10 weeks and is evidenced by depression, sleep disturbance, fatigue, chills, and muscle pain.
3. Third phase. This phase is characterized by craving for cocaine, which possibly contributes to relapse for months following abstinence.

The drugs investigated in the treatment of cocaine are utilized to reduce cocaine craving by restoring neurotransmitter imbalances (Rao *et al.*, 1995). Dopamine agonists, bromocriptine, and amantadine have been employed with mixed results (i.e., some studies have supported the effective use of the medication, some have not) (Rao *et al.*, 1995). Tricyclic antidepressants such as desipramine and imipramine have also yielded mixed results (Rao *et al.*, 1995). Serotonergic agents, gluoxetine and sertraline, show some promise in reducing craving and elevating mood (Rao *et al.*, 1995). The mixed opioid agonist–antagonist, buprenorphine, may be helpful in reducing cocaine craving, but there is some concern about abuse potential; this drug may be particularly helpful for those patients who abuse cocaine and opioids together (Gold & Miller, 1995; Kleber, 1995; Rao *et al.*, 1995). Studies of the antiseizure medication carbamazepine have revealed inconclusive results (Rao *et al.*, 1995). Neuroleptic medications such as haloperidol have been shown to antagonize the use of cocaine, but toxicity and side effects are problematic (Rao *et al.*, 1995). The opioid antagonist, naltrexone, has demonstrated efficacy for reduction of alcohol use and shows some promise for reduction of cocaine use (Kleber, 1995; Rao *et al.*, 1995). Finally, disulfiram, a medication with proven success in reducing alcohol use, may be helpful in reducing cocaine use in those patients abusing both alcohol and cocaine (Kleber, 1995).

Alcohol

Primary medications employed for withdrawal from alcohol are benzodiazepines, especially the intermediate-term acting medications, such as chlordiazepoxide and diazepam (Gold & Miller, 1995).

The aversive agent, disulfiram (Antabuse), has been used to maintain abstinence. When alcohol is consumed with disulfiram, a toxic reaction is precipitated. This is a very effective treatment when the disulfiram is taken; the primary problem with disulfiram is compliance (Gold & Miller, 1995). Psychotherapy has been demonstrated to enhance compliance when combined with disulfiram treatment (Gold & Miller, 1995).

Opioids

Withdrawal from opioids has been likened to a case of the flu (American Psychiataric Association, 1994):

1. Dysphoric mood
2. Nausea or vomiting
3. Muscle aches
4. Runny eyes and nose
5. Diarrhea
6. Fever
7. Pupillary dilation
8. Piloerection
9. Sweating

For shorter-acting drugs like heroin, withdrawal symptoms emerge within 6 to 24 hr after last use. Subtle withdrawal symptoms may last for months (protracted withdrawal), contributing to relapse.

Orally administered methadone is the treatment of choice for detoxification from heroin and morphine. Methadone has a longer half-life than heroin and morphine and eases the discomfort of withdrawal (Gold & Miller, 1995; Jaffe, 1995).

Methadone is also used as a maintenance agent for opioid dependence. Use of methadone has been associated with reductions in illicit opioid abuse, HIV infection, criminal behavior, and an increase in social rehabilitation (Bertschy, 1995). Psychotherapy and counseling are vital components of methadone maintenance treatments (Bertschy, 1995; Hagman, 1994; Reilly *et al.*, 1995). Treatment retention and compliance, as well as other positive outcomes, are strongly related to the provision of medical and psychosocial services (e.g., individual and group therapies, education, relapse prevention training, family counseling, and involvement in 12-step programs) (Bertschy, 1995; Hagman, 1994; Reilly *et al.*, 1995).

Two factors are crucial for retention of patients in methadone maintenance treatment: length of time of detoxification and dose of methadone. Specifically, longer detoxification models (e.g., the 180-day versus the standard 21-day model) and higher doses of methadone (i.e., 60 mg to 100 mg per day or more if necessary) are associated with positive outcomes (Bertschy, 1995). Studies support the practice of maintaining patients in treatment until they stabilize on methadone, desire detoxification, and participate in significant support services. A minority of patients (5 to 20%) remain on methadone maintenance for 10 or more years. Methadone maintenance treatment appears to yield best results for older patients (above 25 years of age) with shorter addiction histories and less frequent criminal behavior (Bertschy, 1995).

Opioid antagonists, naltrexone and naloxone, have been used to precipitate rapid detoxification and as maintenance agents (Gold & Miller, 1995; Jaffe, 1995). As antagonists, naltrexone and naloxone effectively block the effects of opioids in the body. Detoxification from opioids typically takes from 5 to 10 days. With the introduction of naltrexone, detoxification can be achieved in 5 days or less (Jaffe, 1995). Naltrexone is often paired with the medication clonidine to soften the discomfort of rapid detoxification. The rationale for rapid detoxification is that some individuals cannot tolerate slow detoxification and do better with an expedited withdrawal (Jaffe, 1995). As maintenance agents, the antagonists are effective for those who are compliant with the medication; however, dropout rates are very high in studies using naltrexone (Jaffe, 1995). Therefore, use of antagonists may be most effective for highly motivated individuals seeking treatment.

Levomethadyl acetate, L-Alpha Acetylmethadol (LAAM), is a medication that has been used for detoxification and maintenance of opioid dependent patients. LAAM has the advantage over methadone in that it has a very long half-life; LAAM only has to be taken every 3 days, rather than daily as is the case with methadone. However, LAAM is not as effective at suppressing withdrawal symptoms and is poorly tolerated by patients. Buprenorphine, the partial agonist–antagonist, has been employed as a detoxification agent; buprenorphine is not as effective as methadone in the suppression of withdrawal symptoms. It is also very poorly tolerated by patients and results in low compliance rates (Jaffe, 1995).

Nicotine

Pharmacological treatment for nicotine abuse consists primarily of aversive agents (Hughes, 1993; Miller & Cocores, 1991; Miller *et al.*, 1991), nicotine replacement, and nonnicotine attenuation of withdrawal symptoms (Brigham, Henningfield, & Stitzer, 1990–1991; Hughes, 1993; Miller & Cocores, 1991; Miller *et al.*, 1991).

Silver acetate lozenges have been employed as aversive agents to deter smoking (Miller & Cocores, 1991; Miller *et al.*, 1991). The lozenges are available without a prescription. When silver acetate interacts with a smoked cigarette, it causes the smoker to experience a bitter taste, thereby deterring smoking behavior. The efficacy of silver acetate as an abstinence-supporting agent is not established (Hughes, 1993).

Nicotine replacement strategies are the most commonly employed pharmacological treatments for nicotine dependence. It has been demonstrated that cigarette smoking decreases following the administration of nicotine (Miller *et al.*, 1991), apparently due to the suppression of withdrawal symptoms. Nicotine is administered via nicotine polacrilex (i.e., nicotine gum) or a transdermal nicotine patch (Hughes, 1993). Hughes's (1993) review of nicotine replacement treatment yielded the following conclusions:

1. Nicotine gum is moderately effective in increasing the cigarette quit rate, but effects are significantly enhanced when combined with counseling.
2. Nicotine gum appears especially beneficial for smokers who are heavily dependent on nicotine.
3. Transdermal nicotine patches appear superior to nicotine gum alone, but not superior when counseling is used with both.
4. Limitations of nicotine gum use include poor compliance, the need for instruction on its proper use, and social acceptability.
5. Nicotine transdermal patches have the advantage of once-daily application, social acceptance, easy use, and the provision of more reliable and steady dosing of nicotine. Treatment compliance is higher for the patch than for nicotine gum.

More recently, nasal spray systems have been developed to deliver nicotine; the strengths and weaknesses of this method of nicotine replacement are currently being studied.

Attenuation of withdrawal effects via a nonnicotine agent has been attempted with clonidine (Miller *et al.*, 1991). The use of clonidine for nicotine treatment does not appear widely supported. The antidepressant agent, bupropion hydrochloride (trade name Zyban; also known as Wellbutrin), has also been employed to assist in smoking cessation. Further investigation is necessary to objectively evaluate the efficacy of this physician-prescribed medication as an aid to smoke-cessation treatment. In fact, none of the nonnicotine pharmacological agents have yet proven effective in improving treatment effectiveness over long-term trials (Hajek, 1996).

The study of urges (sometimes referred to as cravings) related to nicotine use serves as a model for understanding the circumscribed role of pharmacotherapy in the treatment of addiction to psychoactive substances. A smoking urge is described as a "subjective experience (with neurobiological concomitants and substrates) representing a motivational state or desire for nicotine, akin to hunger for food" (Shiffman *et al.*, 1997, p. 104); urges may be experienced for all drugs of abuse. The experience of nicotine urges is strongly related to relapse to cigarette smoking. More specifically, urge intensity and duration significantly increase prior to a lapse (Shiffman *et al.*, 1997). It has been erroneously suggested that urges are simply a consequence of withdrawal from nicotine; indeed, pharmacological products purportedly target the "withdrawal" symptom of urging to assist smokers to quit. The natural history of urges, however, contradicts the idea that urges are entirely withdrawal related. For example, the experience of urges is not more intense after cessation of cigarette use; in fact, urge intensity appears to be at its peak during ad lib smoking. Urges appear to be episodic in nature, occurring in response to certain cues. Rather than withdrawal based, urges appear to be evoked through association with internal and external stimuli (Pavlovian conditioning). Cues associated with intense urges include negative affect, smoking cues (e.g., exposure to smokers, cigarette availability, lack of smoking restrictions), and consumption of food and alcohol (Shiffmann *et al.*, 1996).

If urges are not withdrawal phenomena, then attenuation of withdrawal symptoms via nicotine replacement, or other nonnicotine pharmacological agents, cannot be expected to effectively stop smoking by itself. To be certain, the treatment literature indicates that effective treatment strategies appear to combine nicotine replacement and psychological therapies. In particular, psychological therapies that teach relapse prevention and coping skills appear promising (Brigham *et al.*, 1990–1991), as do interventions employing social support (Pirie, Rooney, Pechacek, Lando, & Schmid, 1997).

An interesting question that often confronts a clinician is whether to initiate smoking cessation treatment during treatment for abuse of other substances. In their review of the literature, Sees and Clark (1993) noted that the simultaneous administration of smoking cessation programs did not compromise treatment for other substances. In fact, these authors (Sees & Clark, 1993) reported that abstinence from other substances was enhanced by abstinence from nicotine. Cigarette smoking, in addition to posing its own health risks, is often associated with use of other substances. Continued smoking appears to place abstinent alcohol and drug abusers at elevated risk for relapse (Sees & Clark, 1993).

TREATMENT EFFECTIVENESS/OUTCOME STUDIES

The literature regarding effectiveness of treatment for psychoactive substance use disorders is summarized next with respect to five parameters: therapist factors, patient factors, program services, duration of treatment, and theoretical orientation of the therapist or program.

Therapist Factors

Research suggests that treatment results may be more dependent on the skills of the therapist than on the theoretical orientation of the therapist (discussed in Najavits & Weiss, 1994). Najavits and Weiss (1994) proposed that therapeutic skill may be particularly important in the treatment of substance abusers because these patients are especially difficult to engage and maintain in treatment. The review of outcome studies found significant differences in relapse and dropout rates as a function of the individual therapist. The following characteristics of therapists correlated with effectiveness in treating substance abusing patients (Miller, 1992; Najavits & Weiss, 1994):

1. The ability to establish a positive working relationship
2. Empathy
3. Genuineness

Note that the identified characteristics contrast sharply with the therapist characteristics typical in the confrontational programs still widely used in the treatment of substance abuse.

Patient Factors

Patient characteristics associated with poor treatment outcome are as follows (discussed in McLellan, Grisson, *et al.*, 1993):

1. More severe substance dependence
2. Lower SES
3. More severe psychiatric impairment
4. Neurocognitive deficits

It is well established that substance abuse is associated with neuropsychological dysfunction (Weinstein & Shaffer, 1993). Although much of the neuropsychological dysfunction may be temporary, it can pose significant impediments to treatment. Those cognitive skills necessary to benefit from treatment—attention, concentration, memory, insight, impulse control, planning, social awareness, and conceptual ability—are often disrupted by substance abuse (Weinstein & Shaffer, 1993). Weinstein and Shaffer (1993) emphasized the need to conduct neuropsychological assessments and, if indicated, provide cognitive remediation as part of the substance abuse treatment.

Program Services

McLellan and associates (McLellan, Grisson, 1993) investigated the effectiveness of four private substance abuse treatment programs. They found significant differences among programs that they attributed to the range and quantity of services—that is, the broader the range of services (including provision of medical, family, employment, education, psychiatric, 12-step, individual and group therapy services) and the more frequently services were offered, the better the treatment outcomes.

An often-cited article by Miller and Hester (1986) stated that inpatient treatment is no more effective than outpatient treatment of alcohol abuse. Cummings

(1991) and Pettinati, Meyers, Jensen, Kaplan, and Evans (1993), however, observed that certain substance abuse patients require inpatient treatment. This population includes the approximately 10% of alcohol abusers that need medical detoxification, those more severely dependent, patients who are less socially stable (i.e., the unemployed, those with minimal family–social support), and those with high psychiatric severity.

Duration of Treatment

Duration of treatment is a very important variable that correlates with treatment outcome. Generally, the longer an individual is in treatment, the better the outcome (discussed in Miller, 1992).

Treatment results may be significantly improved if and when appropriate matching factors are identified (patient–treatment matching is further discussed in Chapter 9). In other words, some treatment failure may be more a function of a mismatch between the patient and the treatment program, rather than from issues inherent to the treatment program, the therapist, or the patient.

Theoretical Orientation

Miller (1992) and Rawson (1995) conducted reviews of the treatment outcome literature. Miller (1992) reported treatment results in terms of three categories: (a) those approaches receiving no support from controlled studies, (b) those receiving mixed support, and (c) those receiving consistently positive support. In the first group (no support) are insight-oriented psychotherapies, confrontational counseling, and antipsychotic medication. In the second group (mixed results) are stress management, covert sensitization, and use of disulfiram (Antabuse). In the third group (i.e., consistently positive results) are social skills training, behavioral marital therapy, the community reinforcement approach (CRA), and behavioral self-control training.

Rawson's (1995) review of outcome studies on treatment of abusers of opioids, cocaine, and alcohol yielded similar results to Miller's (1992). Regarding opioid treatment, insight-oriented treatment has no demonstrated effectiveness as a stand-alone treatment. In fact, no psychotherapeutic treatment alone has been shown to be effective for the treatment of an actively abusing or recently abstinent opioid addict.

However, psychotherapies are effective in an adjunctive role to pharmacotherapies and help reduce attrition and enhance treatment compliance with methadone maintenance and naltrexone treatment.

Because there is no pharmacologically effective treatment for cocaine addiction, psychotherapeutic programs represent the treatment of choice. Effective outpatient treatment models include the community reinforcement approach (CRA) and relatively intense multicomponent models such as those developed by Washton and Rawson (both discussed in Rawson, 1995). Both models offer treatment for up to a year and include family and marital therapy, psychoeducation, individual and group therapy, relapse prevention, and 12-step services.

With respect to treatment of alcohol abusers, Rawson (1995) reported no support for traditional, passive, insight-oriented psychotherapy. Social skills training and CRA have produced consistently positive results.

Rawson (1995) reported the following general conclusions regarding the treatment of psychoactive substance use disorders: traditional weekly, insight-oriented treatment is inadequate for individuals in early recovery. Modified approaches, especially those proposing integration with other treatment approaches (Zweben, 1995), may be more effective. Forrest (1985) described a psychoanalytically informed model that requires an active role for the therapist and an explicit focus on addiction as a primary condition. This modified approach appears potentially more effective than traditional psychoanalytic approaches. Relapse prevention, CRA, social skills training, and stress management are effective therapies especially as components of comprehensive treatment programs. Motivational interviewing (client-centered), brief interventions, and network therapy are relatively new but very promising approaches. Finally, patients with Axis I and II psychopathology (according to DSM IV criteria) benefit significantly from psychotherapy when combined with substance abuse treatment.

The value of 12-step programs is confirmed by research. For example, AA and NA attendance are positively associated with abstinence (Johnson & Herringer, 1992; Snow, Prochaska, & Rossi, 1994). Snow and associates (1994) identified specific components of AA they thought were active ingredients in fostering behavior change: control of drinking cues (by avoiding people, places, and things associated with alcohol); the development of healthy relationships; and the emphasis on awareness about alcohol, its effects, and the need to receive help. Those who are strongly involved with AA are more likely to use the AA tools for behavior change. Similarly, Montgomery and colleagues (1995) found that degree of involvement with AA, not simply the number of meetings attended, was associated with positive outcomes. In other words, presence at meetings (e.g., if mandated by a court) does not ensure benefit; meaningful participation in the program is necessary.

ALTERNATIVE TREATMENTS

Two alternative, or nontraditional, treatment approaches represented in the literature are acupuncture and transcendental mediation (TM).

Acupuncture

Acupuncture has been investigated primarily as a detoxification treatment (Brewington, Smith, & Lipton, 1994; McLellan, Grossman, Blaine, & Haverkos, 1993; Washburn *et al.*, 1993). The technique of acupuncture consists of inserting needles into acupuncture points to produce curative effects on organ functioning (Brewington, Smith, & Lipton, 1994). Typically, as a detoxification method, stimulation of the ear is conducted with needles or staples.

Positive findings from acupuncture therapy have been reported in terms of treatment retention, reduction in use, and relief from withdrawal symptoms of opiates, cocaine, alcohol, and tobacco; however, the results are inconclusive due to a lack of methodological rigor and the need to replicate the few well-controlled studies (Brewington *et al.*, 1994; McLellan, Grossman, *et al.*, 1993). The purported mechanism of action in acupuncture techniques is the release of endogenous opiates (Brewington *et al.*, 1994).

Transcendental Meditation (TM)

Transcendental meditation (TM) is a holistic, natural process employed for personal development, promotion of health, and longevity (Brooks, 1994; Gelderloos *et al.*, 1991; Glaser, 1994). Meditation is typically practiced twice a day for approximately 20 min. Gelderloos and colleagues (1991) have pointed out that TM has demonstrated effectiveness for reducing psychological distress and enhancing self-esteem, well-being, and self-empowerment. These positive effects make TM a potentially valuable treatment for substance abuse. The literature review by Gelderloos, Walton, Orme-Johnson, & Alexander (1991) suggests that TM can be helpful as an adjunct to treatment and in prevention of substance abuse. However, the studies reviewed lacked scientific rigor and further evaluation is indicated. Glaser (1994) has reported positive effects from the use of TM in the treatment of substance abusers but concedes that his patients are highly motivated and self-selected to participate in a nontraditional program of treatment. Brooks (1994) also supported the use of TM in the treatment of substance abuse based on clinical experience and not strict scientific study.

Concluding Remarks on Acupuncture and TM

In summary, the success of therapy utilizing acupuncture and TM has achieved some support in the treatment literature. However, these treatments are far from consistently demonstrating efficacy in scientifically valid studies. Acupuncture and TM are generally considered experimental, adjunctive treatment interventions and not first-line methods of treatment for substance abuse.

REFERENCES

Alcoholics Anonymous. (1952). *Twelve steps and twelve traditions*. New York: Alcoholics Anonymous World Services.

American Psychiatric Association. (1994). *Diagnostic and statistical manual of mental disorders* (4th ed.). Washington, DC: Author.

American Society of Addiction Medicine. (1991). *Patient placement criteria for the treatment of psychoactive substance use disorders.* Washington, DC: Author.

Annis, H. M. (1986). A relapse prevention model for treatment of alcoholics. In W. R. Miller & N. Heather (Eds.), *Treating addictive behaviors: Processes of change* (pp. 407–433). New York: Plenum Press.

Azrin, N. H., Sisson, R. W., Meyers, R., & Godley, M. (1982). Alcoholism treatment by disulfiram and community reinforcement therapy. *Journal of Behavior Therapy & Experimental Psychiatry, 13*(2), 105–112.

Baker, L. A., Galea, R. P., Lewis, B. F., Paolantonio, B. A., & Tessier-Woupio, D. T. (1989). Relapse prevention training for drug abusers. *Alcoholism Treatment Quarterly, 6,* 173–208.

Bell, A., & Rollnick, S. (1996). Motivational interviewing in practice: A structured approach. In F. Rotgers, D. S. Keller, & J. Morgenstern (Eds.), *Treating substance abuse: Theory and technique* (pp. 266–285). New York: Guilford Press.

Bertschy, G. (1995). Methadone maintenance treatment: An update. *European Archives of Psychiatry Clinical Neuroscience, 245,* 114–124.

Book, J., Harbin, H., Marques, C., Silverman, C., Lizanich-Aro, S., & Lazarus, A. (1995). The ASAM and Green Spring alcohol and drug detoxification and rehabilitation criteria for utilization and review. *The American Journal on Addictions, 4*(3), 187–197.

Brewington, V., Smith, M., & Lipton, D. (1994). Acupuncture as a detoxification treatment: An analysis of controlled research. *Journal of Substance Abuse Treatment, 11*(4), 289–307.

Brigham, J., Henningfield, J. E., & Stitzer, M. L. (1990–1991). Smoking relapse: A review. *The International Journal of the Addictions, 25*(9A and 10A), 1239–1255.

Brooks, J. (1994). The application of Maharishi Ayur-Veda to mental health and substance abuse treatment. *Alcoholism Treatment Quarterly, 11*(3–4), 395–411.

Brown, R. A. (1980). Conventional education and controlled drinking education courses with convicted drunken drivers. *Behavior Therapy, 11,* 632–642.

Caddy, G. R., & Lovibond, S. H. (1976). Self-regulation and discriminated aversive conditioning in the modification of alcoholics' drinking behavior. *Behavior Therapy, 7,* 223–230.

Carney, M. M., & Kivlahan, D. R. (1995). Motivational subtypes among veterans seeking substance abuse treatment: Profiles based on stages of change. *Psychology of Addictive Behaviors, 9*(2), 135–142.

Carroll, J. F. X. (1992). The evolving American therapeutic community. *Alcoholism Treatment Quarterly, 9*(3–4), 175–181.

Carroll, K. M., Rounsaville, B. J., & Keller, D. S. (1991). Relapse prevention strategies for the treatment of cocaine abuse. *American Journal of Drug Abuse, 17*(3), 19–26.

Cummings, N. A. (1991). Inpatient versus outpatient treatment of substance abuse: Recent developments in the controversy. *Contemporary Family Therapy, 13*(5), 507–520.

Dodgen, C. E. (1994). *What should I know about someone who abuses alcohol or other drugs?* Holmes Beach, FL: Learning Publications.

Forrest, G. G. (1985). Psychodynamically oriented treatment of alcoholism and substance abuse. In T. E. Bratten and G. G. Forrest (Eds.), *Alcoholism and substance abuse: Strategies for clinical intervention* (pp. 307–336). New York: The Free Press.

Galanter, M. (1987). Social network therapy for cocaine dependence. *Advances in Alcohol and Substance Abuse, 6,* 159–175.

Galizio, M., & Maisto, S. A. (Eds.)(1985). *Determinants of substance abuse: Biological, psychological, and environmental factors.* New York: Plenum Press.

Gelderloos, P., Walton, K. G., Orme-Johnson, D. W., & Alexander, C. N. (1991). Effectiveness of the Transcendental Meditation program in preventing and treating substance misuse: A review. *The International Journal of the Addictions, 26*(3), 293–325.

Glaser, J. L. (1994). Clinical applications of Maharishi Ayur-Veda in chemical dependency disorders. *Alcoholism Treatment Quarterly, 11*(3–4), 367–394.

Gold, M. S., & Miller, N. S. (1995). Pharmacological therapies for addiction, withdrawal, and relapse: General aspects. In N. S. Miller & M. S. Gold (Eds.), *Pharmacological therapies for drug & alcohol addictions* (pp. 11–27). New York: Marcel Dekker.

Hagman, G. (1994). Methadone maintenance counseling: Definition, principles, components. *Journal of Substance Abuse Treatment, 11*(5), 405–413.

Hajek,P. (1996). Current issues in behavioral and pharmacological approaches to smoking cessation. *Addictive Behaviors, 21*(6), 699–707.

Higgins, S. T., Budney, A. J., Bickel, W. K., Foerg, F. E., Donham, R., & Badger, G. J. (1994). Incentives improve outcome in outpatient behavioral treatment of cocaine dependence. *Archives of General Psychiatry, 51*, 568–576.

Higgins, S. T., Budney A. J., Bickel, W. K., Hughes, J. R. Foerg, F., & Badger, G. (1993). Achieving cocaine abstinence with a behavioral approach. *American Journal of Psychiatry, 150*(5), 763–769.

Hughes, J. R. (1993). Pharmacotherapy for smoking cessation: Unvalidated assumptions, anomalies, and suggestions for future research. *Journal of Consulting and Clinical Psychology, 61*(5), 751–760.

Jaffe, J. H. (1995). Pharmacological treatment of opioid dependence: Current techniques and new findings. *Psychiatric Annals, 25*(6), 369–375.

Johnson, E., & Herringer, L. G. (1992). A note on the utilization of common support activities and relapse following substance abuse treatment. *The Journal of Psychology, 127*(1), 73–78.

Kadden, R. M., & Mauriello, I. J. (1991). Enhancing participation in substance abuse treatment using an incentive system. *Journal of Substance Abuse, 8*, 113–124.

Khantzian, E. J. (1985). The self-medication hypothesis of addictive disorders: Focus on heroin and cocaine dependence. *American Journal of Psychiatry, 142*(11), 1259–1264.

Khantzian, E. J. (1990). *Group treatment of cocaine dependence—A psychodynamic approach to relapse prevention.* Paper presented at conference on Treating the Addictions. Boston, MA.

Kleber, H. D. (1995). Pharmacotherapy, current and potential, for the treatment of cocaine dependence. *Clinical Neuropharmacology, 18*(S1), S96–S109.

Krystal, H. (1979). Alexithymia and psychotherapy. *American Journal of Psychotherapy, 33*(17), 17–26.

Laberg, J. C. (1990). What is presented, and what prevented, in cue exposure and response prevention with alcohol dependent subjects? *Addictive Behaviors, 15*, 367–386.

Leeds, J., & Morgenstern, J. (1996). Psychoanalytic theories of substance abuse. In F. Rotgers, D. S. Keller, & J. Morgenstern (Eds.), *Treating substance abuse: Theory and technique* (pp. 68–83). New York: Guilford Press.

McCrady, B. S., & Epstein, E. E. (1996). Theoretical bases of family approaches to substance abuse treatment. In F. Rotgers, D. S. Keller, & J. Morgenstern (Eds.), *Treating substance abuse: Theory and technique* (pp. 117–142). New York: Guilford Press.

McDougal, J. (1978). *Plea for a measure of abnormality.* New York: International Universities Press.

McLellan, A. T., Grisson, G. R., Brill, P., Durell, J. Metzger, D. S., & O'Brien, C. P. (1993). Private substance abuse treatments: Are some programs more effective than others? *Journal of Substance Abuse Treatment, 10*, 243–254.

McLellan, T. A., Grossman, D. S., Blaine, J. D., & Haverkos, H. W. (1993). Acupuncture treatment for drug abuse: A technical review. *Journal of Substance Abuse Treatment, 10*, 569–576.

Marlatt, G. A., & Gordon, J. R.(Eds.). (1985). *Relapse prevention: Maintenance strategies in the treatment of addictive behaviors.* New York: Guilford Press.

Miller, N. S., & Cocores, J. A. (1991). Nicotine dependence: Diagnosis, pharmacology, and treatment. *Journal of Addictive Diseases, 11*(2), 51–65.

Miller, N. S., Cocores, J. A., & Belkin, B. B. (1991). Nicotine dependence: Diagnosis, chemistry and pharmacological treatments. *Annals of Clinical Psychiatry, 3*, 47–53.

Miller, W. R. (1992). The effectiveness of treatment for substance abuse: Reasons for optimism. *Journal of Substance Abuse Treatment, 9*, 93–102.

Miller, W. R., & Hester, R. K. (1986). Inpatient alcoholism treatment. *American Psychologist, 41*, 794–805.

Miller, W. R., & Tonigan, J. S. (1996). Assessing drinkers' motivation for change: The Stages of Change Readiness and Treatment Eagerness Scale (SOCRATES). *Psychology of Addictive Behaviors, 10*(2), 81–89.

Montgomery, H. A., Miller, W., & Tonigan, J. S. (1995). Does Alcoholics Anonymous involvement predict treatment outcome? *Journal of Substance Abuse Treatment, 12*(4), 241–246.

Morgenstern, J., & Leeds, J. (1993). Contemporary psychoanalytic theories of substance abuse: A disorder in search of a paradigm. *Psychotherapy, 30*(2), 194–206.

Najavits, L. M., & Weiss, R. D. (1994). Variations in therapist effectiveness in the treatment of patients with substance use disorders: An empirical review. *Addiction, 89*(6), 679–688.

Pettinati, H. M., Meyers, K., Jensen, J. M., Kaplan, F., & Evans, B. D. (1993). Inpatient vs. outpatient treatment for substance dependence revisited. *Psychiatric Quarterly, 64*(2), 173–182.

Pirie, P. L., Rooney, B. L., Pechacek, T. F., Lando, H. A., & Schmid, L. A. (1997). Incorporating social support into a community-wide smoking-cessation contest. *Addictive Behaviors, 22*(1), 131–137.

Platt, J. J., & Husband, S. D. (1993). An overview of problem-solving and social skills approaches in substance abuse treatment. *Psychotherapy, 30*(2), 276–330.

Prochaska, J. O., & DiClemente, C. C. (1986). Toward a comprehensive model of change. In W. R. Miller & N. Heather (Eds.), *Treating addictive behaviors: Processes of change* (pp. 3–27). New York: Plenum Press.

Rao, S., Ziedonis, D., & Kosten, T. (1995). The pharmacotherapy of cocaine dependence. *Psychiatric Annals, 25*(6), 363–368.

Rawson, R. A. (1995). Is psychotherapy effective for substance abusers? In A. M. Washton (Ed.), *Psychotherapy and substance abuse: A practitioner's handbook* (pp. 55–75). New York: Guilford Press.

Rawson, R. A., Obert, J. L., McCann, M. J., & Marinelli Casey, P. (1993a). Relapse prevention models for substance abuse treatment. *Psychotherapy, 30*(2), 284–299.

Rawson, R. A., Obert, J. L., McCann, M. J., & Marinelli-Casey, P. (1993b). Relapse prevention strategies in outpatient substance abuse treatment. *Psychology of Addictive Behaviors, 7*(2), 85–95.

Reilly, P. M., Banys, P., Tusel, D. J., Sees, K. L., Krumenaker, C. L., & Shopshire, M. S. (1995). Methadone transition treatment: A treatment model for 180-day methadone detoxification. *The International Journal of the Addictions, 30*(4), 387–402.

Roffman, R. A., & Barnhart, R. (1987). Assessing need for marijuana dependence treatment through an anonymous telephone interview. *International Journal of Addictions, 22*(7), 639–651.

Rotgers, F. (1996). Behavioral theory of substance abuse treatment: Bringing science to bear on practice. In F. Rotgers, D. S. Keller, & J. Morgenstern (Eds.), *Treating substance abuse: Theory and technique* (pp. 174–201). New York: Guilford Press.

Sees, K. L., & Clark, W. (1993). When to begin smoking cessation in substance abusers. *Journal of Substance Abuse, 10,* 189–195.

Shiffman, S., Engberg, J. B., Paty, J. A., Perz, W. G., Gnys, M., Kassel, J. D., & Hickcox, M. (1997). A day at a time: Predicting smoking lapse from daily urge. *Journal of Abnormal Psychology, 106*(1), 104–116.

Shiffman, S., Gnys, M., Richards, T. J., Paty, J. A. Hickocox, M., & Kassel, J. D. (1996). Temptations to smoke after quitting: A comparison of lapsers and maintainers. *Health Psychology, 15*(6), 455–461.

Snow, M. G., Prochaska, J. O., & Rossi, J. S. (1994). Processes of change in Alcoholics Anonymous: Maintenance factors in long-term sobriety. *Journal of Studies on Alcohol, 55,* 362–371.

Wallace, B. C. (1989). Relapse prevention in psychoeducational groups for compulsive crack cocaine smokers. *Journal of Substance Abuse Treatment, 6,* 229–239.

Walton, M. A., Castro, F. G., & Barrington, E. H. (1994). The role of attributions in abstinence, lapse, and relapse following substance abuse treatment. *Addictive Behaviors, 19*(3), 319–331.

Washburn, A. M., Fullilove, R. E., Fullilove, M. T., Keenan, P. A., McGee, B., Morris, K. A., Sorensen, J. L., & Clark, W. W. (1993). Acupuncture heroin detoxification: A single-blind clinical trial. *Journal of Substance Abuse Treatment, 10,* 345–351.

Washton, A. M. (1989). *Cocaine abuse: Treatment, recovery, and relapse prevention.* New York: Norton.

Weinstein, C. S., & Shaffer, H. J. (1993). Neurocognitive aspects of substance abuse treatment: A psychotherapist's primer. *Psychotherapy, 30*(2), 317–332.

Wexler, H. K. (1995). The success of therapeutic communities for substance abusers in American prisons. *Journal of Psychoactive Drugs, 27*(1), 57–65.

Wurmser, L. (1981). Psychodynamics of substance abuse. In J. H. Lowinson & P. Ruiz (Eds.), *Substance abuse: Clinical problems and perspectives* (pp. 63–77). Baltimore: Williams & Wilkins.

Zweben, J. E. (1995). Integrating psychotherapy and 12-step approaches. In A. M. Washton (Ed.), *Psychotherapy and substance abuse: A practitioner's handbook* (pp. 124–140). New York: Guilford Press.

9

TREATMENT II: PLANNING, IMPLEMENTING, AND MANAGING TREATMENT AND THE COURSE OF RECOVERY

PHASES OF RECOVERY

Two illustrative phase or stage models of recovery are described by Wallace (1992) and Rounsaville (1995). Wallace (1992) described three phases of recovery, each requiring different tasks of the patient and therapist. She suggested that awareness of phase-specific issues can help provide a good fit between patient readiness and clinical interventions. Wallace's (1992) model is presented here:

1. Phase I (withdrawal phase). This phase spans Days 1 through 14 of initial abstinence. Primary clinical tasks are assessment, stabilization, treatment retention, motivation enhancement, and relapse prevention.

2. Phase II (prolonging abstinence). This phase spans the first 6 months of abstinence. Clinical tasks are continuing assessment, reducing risk of relapse, sustaining motivation, supporting ego functioning, and improving self-regulation.

3. Phase III (pursuing lifetime recovery). This phase spans from 6 months and beyond. Clinical tasks are continuing assessment, fostering a stable drug-free lifestyle, relapse prevention, addressing other psychopathology, and continuing improvement of self-regulation.

Rounsaville (1995) described three stages of treatment:

1. Abstinence initiation. During abstinence initiation intensive treatment facilitates the development of new ways to behave and think. During this initial phase of treatment, multidimensional assessments are conducted and corresponding multidimensional treatment options are offered. Treatment recommendations are adapted to the patient's stage of motivation. It is recommended that less intensive treatment be attempted first and that both pharmacotherapy and psychotherapy be employed (Rounsaville, 1995; Zweben, 1993b).

2. Relapse prevention. Relapse prevention consists of formal relapse prevention training and the consolidation of therapeutic gains.

3. Managing relapse. Relapse management refers to the process of analyzing precipitants and consequences of relapse and adjusting treatment accordingly. When serious relapse occurs, treatment intensity should be increased. However, it is not recommended that previous treatment interventions simply be repeated. Rather, changes in modality (e.g., adding family therapy to individual therapy) or setting (from outpatient to intensive outpatient) should be considered.

RELAPSE PARAMETERS

Marlatt and Gordon's (1985) work on relapse is seminal. They report that about two-thirds of all initial lapses occur within the first 90 days of initiation of abstinence. Relapse rates stabilize after 90 days of abstinence. Overall, 80% of those initiating abstinence relapse within 1 year. However, if 1 year of abstinence is achieved, there is an 80% chance of achieving a second year of abstinence (Rounsaville, 1995).

In their study of precipitants of relapse, Marlatt and Gordon (1985) identified three high-risk situations that accounted for nearly three-fourths of relapses:

1. Negative (unpleasant) emotional state (35%)
2. Social pressure (20%) to use
3. Interpersonal conflicts (16%)

TREATMENT GOALS

Traditional Abstinence Goals

There was at one time, not long ago, a raging controversy over what should be appropriate treatment goals for substance abusers. The controversy centered on whether abstinence was a necessary requirement for recovery or if controlled use was an appropriate alternative. A thorough reading of the current literature reveals little evidence of such division of opinions among those conducting treatment and research. At this time, the most widely accepted goal–requirement of treatment is complete abstinence. Abstinence is necessary both to arrest the destructive processes associated with abuse and to arrive at an accurate diagnosis—that is, in order to assess comorbidity, abstinence is necessary (Washton, 1995). Also, if a person is unable to achieve abstinence upon entering treatment, certain recommendations to help achieve abstinence would follow (Washton, 1995).

Controlled Use of Alcohol

Notable exceptions to the traditional approach (requiring abstinence) are those that adhere to strict behavioral approaches (e.g., Rotgers, 1996). It is noteworthy that controlled use goals are usually attempted with alcohol abusers, not abusers of other substances. Some clinicians, however, believe that abstinence from all substances is too rigorous an initial requirement for the severely dually impaired (e.g., Zweben, 1993a). Even those who feel controlled drinking is a reasonable goal recommend abstinence for patients exhibiting the following characteristics:

1. The patient has ever met the diagnostic criteria for dependence.
2. The patient has experienced previous unsuccessful attempts of controlled use.
3. Unsafe work conditions exist (e.g., the patient is a truck driver or an airline pilot).
4. Life-threatening circumstances exist (e.g., the patient is suicidal).

DETOXIFICATION

A clinician often needs to assess whether medical detoxification is necessary for substance abusers. The most prudent course of action is to refer patients to a physician for evaluation (Washton, 1995). The most severe withdrawal syndromes occur with alcohol, other central nervous system depressants, and opioids; stimulants result in a significant but less severe abstinence reaction although cocaine withdrawal does not require medical detoxification (Carroll, 1996). If no alcohol or drug use has occurred in the previous 2 to 3 weeks, the need for medical detoxification is unlikely (Washton, 1995).

Abrupt withdrawal from alcohol and other central nervous system depressants can be fatal; detoxification from opioids is very uncomfortable, but it is usually not dangerous (Washton, 1995). In most cases (approximately 90%), outpatient detoxification of alcohol is appropriate. Exceptions to outpatient detoxification of alcohol include the following (Washton, 1995):

1. A history of seizures
2. Prior experience of delirium tremens
3. Presence of medical complications (e.g., cardiac condition)
4. Inability of the patient to comply with the medication schedule

Alcohol withdrawal is usually managed with barbiturates or long-acting benzodiazepines (Carroll, 1996). Withdrawal from other central nervous system depressants is usually accomplished by tapering doses of a drug within the same class with a longer half-life than the one the person is addicted to (Carroll, 1996). Methadone, LAAM, and the combination of naltrexone and clonidine are used for detoxification from opioids (Carroll, 1996) (discussed in detail in Chapter 8).

ENGAGEMENT OF PATIENTS IN TREATMENT

It has been demonstrated that greater length of time in treatment and compliance with recommendations are associated with positive treatment outcomes. Therefore, patient engagement in treatment is of paramount importance (Simpson, Joe, Rowan-Szal, & Greener, 1995). The current thinking on patient engagement represents a significant departure from the views of traditional substance abuse models. Rather than aggressively confronting a patient's denial, clinicians now acknowledge and address the inevitability of patient ambivalence (e.g., Washton, 1995). The approach of client-centered treatment (motivational interviewing) is gaining increasing acceptance for its success in helping patients to establish trust, fostering a positive working relationship, and maintaining the patient in treatment.

CLIENT–TREATMENT MATCHING

Given the heterogeneity of substance abusers as a group, that one type of treatment would not be best for all substance abusers seems self-evident. As an obvious example, relatively low-intensity outpatient treatment may be perfectly appropriate for an employed, married, nonphysically dependent cocaine abuser. However, such treatment would be grossly inadequate for an unemployed, homeless, physically dependent opioid abuser. Client–treatment matching, therefore, is an accepted concept. Determining an appropriate treatment plan after assessing specific client needs is both clinically effective and cost-effective (Del Boca & Mattson, 1994).

Client–treatment matching involves systematic assignment of clients to various treatment alternatives based on identified client characteristics and predetermined matching guidelines (Del Boca & Mattson, 1994). The problem, of course, is identifying the relevant client characteristics on which to make a matching decision and to find the best treatment match. Client matching characteristics that have been studied for alcohol abuse are age, minority status, gender, dependence severity, degree of psychopathology, and quality of social support (Del Boca & Mattson, 1994). On the treatment side, different modalities (e.g., group, individual or family therapies), type of psychotherapy (e.g., cognitive–behavioral, psychodynamic), intensity and duration of treatment, setting (e.g., inpatient versus outpatient), stage of treatment, and therapist factors (e.g., gender, recovery status) have been investigated (Del Boca & Mattson, 1994).

Client–treatment matching research is still in the preliminary stages and additional study is needed to establish valid matching schemes that can be employed in practice.

Project Match

A major study sponsored by the National Institute on Alcohol Abuse and Alcoholism (NIAAA) is Project Match (described in Del Boca & Mattson, 1994). Results from the study were recently reported (American Psychological Association, 1997). In this study, subjects were randomly assigned to one of three psychosocial treatment groups: 12-step, cognitive–behavioral, and motivation-enhancement. Subjects received 12 weeks of treatment and were followed for a year of posttreatment. Factors were analyzed to determine whether certain variables predicted response to treatment. All treatment approaches resulted in positive outcomes. The results generally supported the efficacy of psychosocial treatments; all treatments reportedly worked equally well.

TREATMENT OF FAMILY MEMBERS OF SUBSTANCE ABUSERS

Inclusion of family members in the treatment of substance abusers contributes to successful treatment results. Family support of treatment lowers attrition and enhances compliance of substance abusers. In addition, family members often are physically, sexually, and emotionally damaged by living with substance abusers and require treatment themselves. Norton (1994) discussed the malignant dynamics often present in families of substance abusers such as family denial, inhumane treatment, inconsistency, and collusion in the substance abuser's faulty reality testing. Because of these experiences, family members, especially children, often experience helplessness, loss of self-esteem, and diminished self-respect (Norton, 1994). Family members are at risk for psychological problems and should also be assessed for indications for treatment.

Adolescent substance abusers, necessarily dependent on their families, present additional clinical concerns. Family risk factors associated with adolescent substance abuse include parental substance abuse, low levels of bonding within the family, and poor parenting skills (discussed in Bukstein, 1995). More positive family functioning pretreatment is associated with better treatment outcome (Friedman, Terras, Kreisher, 1995). With adolescents, family treatment is necessary to improve interpersonal communication, address addiction of parents if present, and assist parents in setting limits and providing appropriate structure (Bukstein, 1995).

Treatment modalities employed to assist families include traditional family therapies, multifamily therapy (providing support and education), and behavior therapies (providing parenting skills training) (Bukstein, 1995).

LINKAGE OF SERVICES

Substance abusing patients often require a range of medical and psychosocial services to address their medical, emotional, social, psychological, spiritual, and economic problems (Edmunds, 1993). If a clinician is working within a comprehensive program or agency, coordination of services may not pose much of a problem. However, clinicians, especially those in private practice, often function in relative isolation from other agencies and programs serving patients (e.g., child abuse/protective agencies, housing, criminal justice, welfare–social services, community health services, and community mental health services). Therefore, services are usually not well integrated.

As a consequence of problems in coordinating services, patients may "fall through the cracks" or receive contradictory and confusing information from different service providers (Edmunds, 1993). Edmunds (1993) underscored the importance of the well-coordinated provision of services and offers several suggestions designed to enhance the linkage of services for substance abusing patients through informal and formal means. Informal ways to enhance the network of various organizations and professionals include regular lunchtime seminars or the joint sponsorship of a public lecture series. Development of a directory of service providers is another way to inform consumers, and various agencies and professionals, of sources of assistance for substance abusers. Edmunds (1993) also recommended that clinicians be aware of self-help groups in their geographic area. Formal relationships between independent service providers can be entered into with written agreements, thereby explicitly linking services.

TREATMENT OF CRIMINAL OFFENDERS

The discussion of treatment of criminal offenders addresses driving-related offenders (DUI, DWI) and substance abusers incarcerated for other offenses.

Driving-Related Offenders

Siegal (1990) (see also Siegal & Cole, 1993) described the evolution of programs designed to treat impaired drivers. Initially, programs relied exclusively on educational techniques. For example, a popular program, the Phoenix Model, consisted of 12 hr of alcohol and driving education. The second generation of interventions consisted of short-term rehabilitation programs known as Power-Motivational Training (PMT). These programs included relaxation training, teaching of communication skills, and assisting the offender to recognize and cope with high-risk situations. Neither the purely educational nor the PMT approaches were effective in reducing DWI (driving while intoxicated) recidivism or alcohol-related automobile accidents. A partial explanation for the failure of these approaches may stem from the lack of individualization of treatment; driving-related offenders are a very diverse group (Veneziano & Veneziano, 1992).

A current model of treatment for driving-related offenders is called the Weekend Intervention Program (WIP) (Siegal, 1990; Siegal, & Cole, 1993). The WIP represents the collaborative efforts of the criminal justice system and substance abuse treatment agencies; it is a court-mandated, 3-day residential program. There are three specific components to WIP: (a) assessment/diagnosis, (b) gentle confrontation of denial, and (c) enhancement of motivation to follow-up with treatment referrals. Due to the short duration of the program (i.e., 3 days), the unrealistic goal of behavioral change is not pursued. Rather, those identified in the assessment phase as requiring substance abuse treatment are referred for follow-up treatment. Only about 50% of first time DWI offenders have a significant substance abuse problem. To adequately address the needs of DWI offenders, intervention programs must be capable of assessing the magnitude of participants' substance abuse problems and directing them to appropriate treatment. The WIP appears to reduce DWI recidivism, especially when coupled with punitive measures such as license suspension (Siegal, 1990).

Treatment of the Incarcerated

Increasing numbers of criminal offenders are drug involved, creating overcrowding in jails and prisons (Peters, Kearns, Murrin, Dolente, & May, 1993). The needs of these criminal offenders are creating a demand for substance abuse services for the incarcerated. Substance abuse treatment in prison is one way to reduce drug use and criminal recidivism. For example, Peters and colleagues (1993) implemented a 6-week, jail-based program that provided group treatment from a cognitive–behavioral, skills-based approach and a focus on relapse prevention. They found that those participants in the treatment program were less likely to be rearrested, remained in the community for longer periods of time before rearrest, and spent less time in jail compared to untreated inmates.

Diverting drug-abusing offenders to community-based treatment programs, as an alternative to incarceration, can also reduce recidivism and correction costs (Anglin & Hser, 1991). Anglin and Hser (1991) identified several crucial characteristics of a community-based treatment model: provision of long-term treatment, a high degree of structure including urine monitoring, an individualized orientation, formal monitoring of outcome, inclusion of services such as medical and psychosocial services, and effective coordination with the criminal justice system.

SELF-HELP GROUPS

Alcoholics Anonymous (AA) and Narcotics Anonymous (NA)

Alcoholics Anonymous (AA) and Narcotics Anonymous (NA) (discussed in Chapter 8) are the most well-known 12-step programs but are by no means the only 12-step programs; nor are NA and AA the only self-help programs for substance abusers.

AL-ANON and ALATEEN/NAR-ANON and NARATEEN

AL-ANON and ALATEEN are 12-step programs that assist family members and friends of alcoholics (AL-ANON Family Groups, 1964). ALATEEN targets younger family members. Analogous to AA, these are group-based, self-help programs that offer support, and education about the disease model of addiction and pathological family dynamics. The 12-steps serve as a pathway to recovery and sanity. Also, as with AA, there are no financial barriers to participation and group meetings are available in almost any community. NAR-ANON and NARATEEN, derivatives of AL-ANON and ALATEEN, are programs organized for family members and friends of drug abusers.

Women for Sobriety

Women for Sobriety is a national, self-help program for women substance abusers only (Women for Sobriety, 1993). The program addresses the special needs of recovering women, including building self-esteem and self-worth and the mitigation of guilt and humiliation. The program is based on the following processes: positive thinking, meditation, group dynamics, and pursuit of health through nutrition. The literature (Women for Sobriety, 1993) describes six levels of recovery and, rather than 12-steps, employs 13 self-statements to assist women in their recovery.

Rational Recovery

Rational Recovery (also referred to as Smart Recovery) is a national, self-help program based on rational emotive therapy rather than the traditional 12-steps of AA (Trimpey, 1990). Rational Recovery represents an alternative to the disease model and is less restrictive than AA (Galanter, Egelko, & Edwards, 1993). In a departure from the AA philosophy, abstinence is not required.

REFERENCES

AL-ANON Family Groups. (1964). *Freedom from despair*. New York: AL-ANON Family Groups.

American Psychological Association. (1997). Tailoring treatments for alcoholics is not the answer. *The APA Monitor, 28*(2), 6.

Anglin, M. D., & Hser, Y. (1991). Criminal justice and the drug-abusing offender: Policy issues of coerced treatment. *Behavioral Sciences and the Law, 9*, 243–267.

Bukstein, O. G. (1995). *Adolescent substance abuse: Assessment, prevention, and treatment*. New York: Wiley & Sons.

Carroll, K. M. (1996). Integrating psychotherapy and pharmacotherapy in substance abuse treatment. In F. Rotgers, D. Keller, & J. Morgenstern (Eds.). *Treating substance abuse: Theory and technique* (pp. 286–318). New York: Guilford Press.

Del Boca, F. K., & Mattson, M. E. (1994). Developments in alcoholism treatment research: Patient-treatment matching. *Alcohol, 11*(6), 471–475.

Edmunds, M. (1993). Resources for linkage of primary health care and substance abuse services. *Journal of Adolescent Chemical Dependency, 2*(3–4), 9–17.

Friedman, A. S., Terras A., & Kreisher, C. (1995). Family and client characteristics as predictors of outpatient treatment outcome for adolescent drug abusers. *Journal of Substance Abuse, 7*, 345–356.

Galanter, M., Egelko, S., & Edwards, H. (1993). Rational recovery: Alternative to AA for addiction? *American Journal of Drug and Alcohol Abuse, 19*(4), 499–510.

Marlatt, G. A., & Gordon, J. R. (Eds.). (1985). *Relapse prevention: Maintenance strategies in the treatment of addictive behaviors*. New York: Guilford Press.

Norton, J. H. (1994). Addiction and family issues. *Alcohol, 11*(6), 457–460.

Peters, R. H., Kearns, W. D., Murrin, M. R., Dolente, A. D., & May, R. L., II. (1993). Examining the effectiveness of in-jail substance abuse treatment. *Journal of Offender Rehabilitation, 19*(3–4), 1–39.

Rotgers, F. (1996). Behavioral theory of substance abuse treatment: Bringing science to bear on practice. In F. Rotgers, D. S. Keller, & J. Morgenstern (Eds.), *Treating substance abuse: Theory and technique* (pp. 174–201). New York: Guilford Press.

Rounsaville, B. J. (1995). *The treatment of alcoholism: Initiating abstinence and preventing relapse with pharmacotherapy and psychotherapy*. (Audiotape). Merrifield, VA: Value Behavioral Health.

Siegal, H. A. (1990). The intervention approach: How it works and its impact. *Alcohol, Drugs and Driving, 6*(3–4), 161–168.

Siegal, H. A., & Cole, P. A. (1993). Enhancing criminal justice based treatment through the application of the intervention approach. *Journal of Drug Issues, 22*, 131–142.

Simpson, D. D., Joe, G. W., Rowan-Szal, G., & Greener, J. (1995). Client engagement and change during drug abuse treatment. *Journal of Substance Abuse, 7*, 117–134.

Trimpey, J. (1990). *Rational recovery from alcoholism: The small book*. Lotus, CA: Lotus Press.

Veneziano, C., & Veneziano, L. (1992). Psychosocial characteristics of persons convicted of driving while intoxicated. *Psychological Reports, 70*, 1123–1130.

Wallace, B. C. (1992). Treatment and recovery in an evolving field. In B. C. Wallace (Ed.), *The chemically dependent: Phases of treatment and recovery* (pp. 3–14). New York: Brunner/Mazel.

Washton, A. M. (1995). Clinical assessment of psychoactive substance abuse. In A. M. Washton (Ed.), *Psychotherapy and substance abuse: A practitioner's handbook* (pp. 23–54). New York: Guilford Press.

Women for Sobriety (1993). *Women & Addictions*. Quakertown, PA: Women for Sobriety.

Zweben, J. E. (1993a). Dual diagnosis: Key issues for the 1990s. *Psychology of Addictive Behaviors, 7*(3), 168–172.

Zweben, J. E. (1993b). Recovery oriented psychotherapy: A model for addiction treatment. *Psychotherapy, 30*(2), 259–268.

10

ISSUES IN SPECIFIC POPULATIONS

The terms subpopulation and special population describe various subdivisions of drug and alcohol-abusing groups. Misunderstanding or lack of consideration of variables such as gender, race, psychiatric comorbidity, culture, age, or occupation, and other differences may create or support barriers to the identification and treatment of substance abusers (Closser & Blow, 1993). Awareness of ethnocultural issues is a significant facet of client–treatment matching (discussed in Chapter 9). This chapter reviews several subpopulations and the issues relevant to psychoactive substance use disorders of each group.

IMPAIRED PHYSICIANS

Definition and Risk Factors

Impaired physician is a term used by the American Medical Association (AMA) to refer to "members of the medical profession whose professional performance is adversely affected by reason of mental illness, alcohol or drug dependence" (Centrella, 1994, p. 91). Although early investigators reported highly elevated addiction rates for physicians, the current thinking is that prevalence rates of substance abuse among physicians are similar to those of other professionals (Centrella, 1994; McAuliffe *et al.*, 1991).

A number of risk factors contribute to physician substance abuse including, primarily, access and familiarity with drugs, and stress (Centrella, 1994). Not surprisingly, personality factors that predate medical training and practice play an important role in the process. Psychosocial factors such as poor coping skills, narcissistic and grandiose personality styles, early deprivation (due to family dysfunction), adjustment problems, and unsatisfactory social and marital relationships contribute to physician vulnerability to substance abuse (Arana, 1982; Richman, 1992). Also, as a group, physicians tend not to ask for help, especially for emotional or behavioral problems. The focus on the needs of others may contribute to neglect of self.

Treatment of Physicians

There are factors that complicate the treatment of physicians. In addition to the denial of their need for help, physicians may be manipulative in treatment, expect special treatment, act aloof from other patients, resist assuming the patient role, and evoke discomfort in treatment professionals (who are uncomfortable about treating a peer) (Arana, 1982).

Substance abusing physicians are most likely to benefit from programs that provide formal, structured, long-term treatment (Centrella, 1994). The following are components of effective treatment of physicians: (a) formal, structured substance abuse treatment program, (b) AA/NA participation, (c) monitored urines, (d) family involvement, and (e) frequent contact with the director of impaired physicians in the respective state (Carlson, Dilts, & Radcliff, 1994; Centrella, 1994).

ETHNIC MINORITIES

Prevalence and Etiological Factors

Research demonstrates that ethnic minorities report disproportionately high rates of drug and alcohol-related problems (Closser & Blow, 1993). Further, traditional treatment approaches do not appear to be as effective and receive lower satisfaction ratings among minority group members (Closser & Blow, 1993; Terrell, 1993). The high incidence of substance abuse among minority groups may reflect elevated stress from several sources (Schinke, Moncher, Palleja, Zayas, & Schilling, 1988):

1. Environmental stressors such as noise, poor housing, crowding, and unsafe conditions
2. Social stressors such as poverty, exposure to drugs, unemployment, and racial discrimination
3. Cognitive stressors such as low self-esteem and perceptions of helplessness

In addition to these stressors, the resources and opportunities to counteract stress are frequently not as readily available in lower income minority communities—social support and coping skills may be taxed by the demands of socioeconomic survival (Terrell, 1993).

The link between education and risk of substance abuse among certain minority groups can be examined by considering the special problems of young Hispanics (Schinke *et al.*, 1988). The vulnerability of Hispanic youth to substance abuse is revealed in the statistic that fewer than 50% are likely to finish high school (Schinke et al, 1988). Consequently, the potential for an environmental support system afforded by the school is lost. A successful school experience enhances earning potential, social competence, and mobility. School failure may create or sustain feelings of inferiority or alienation, which in turn may foster Hispanic youths' substance abuse behavior (Schinke *et al.*, 1988).

Cultural Influences on Substance Abuse

Cultural and ethnic traditions exert some influence on the use of substances. Most cultures endorse rules about the use or control of substances (Westermeyer, 1995). When movement occurs from one culture to another (e.g., through migration, occupation, or marriage) the original rules or constraints may be lost or in conflict with the norms of the dominant culture (Terrell, 1993). Weak acculturation can also result in inadequate internalization of values, norms, and customs about the control of substance use. Acculturation is a process whereby individuals "acquire the values, norms, and skills that enable them to live congenially with their cultural group" (Westermeyer, 1995, p. 593). Difficulties in acculturation can be caused by substance-abusing or psychiatrically impaired parents, poor role models, and a paucity of constructive contact between parent and child.

Treatment of Ethnic Minorities

Given the important influence of culture on substance use, it is no surprise that awareness and inclusion of cultural values in treatment improves program effectiveness with minority populations (Terrell, 1993; Westermeyer, 1995). It is important to note that even within a given subgroup (e.g., African American, Hispanic) there is significant heterogeneity so that no single best approach exists; rather, a general sensitivity and flexibility about incorporation of cultural beliefs and concepts fosters recovery (Closser & Blow, 1993). Including culture-specific values in treatment enhances credibility and relevance, increases pride and self-esteem, and reduces acculturation stress (Terrell, 1993).

Barriers to Treatment for Ethnic Minorities

Access barriers to treatment may be external (e.g., transportation to treatment program, cost of treatment) or internal (e.g., denial, shame). Barriers for Hispanic substance abusers include the following (Westermeyer, 1995):

1. Language
2. Financial limitations
3. An absence of role models at the treatment programs

Allen (1995) identified the following access barriers for African American women:

1. Responsibilities at home as wife and mother
2. Cost of treatment/lack of insurance
3. Perceived need for substances to cope with everyday stress
4. Fear of loss of children
5. Shame

To achieve success with minority populations, treatment programs must respond to the identified barriers to treatment and include culture-specific concepts. For example, the strong family orientation of Hispanic culture should be recognized and utilized in strengthening the social support network (Schinke *et al.*, 1988). For Native Americans, the promotion of bicultural competence, which integrates the positive values of both cultures, may prove helpful (Terrell, 1993). The inclusion of culture-specific factors in treatment possesses intuitive appeal, but experimental research is needed to corroborate treatment success.

WOMEN

Prevalence of Substance Abuse

Women demonstrate a lower prevalence of alcohol abuse than men, although the rate of abuse significantly increased from the early 1980s to the early 1990s (Closser & Blow, 1993). Women are more significantly affected by alcohol than men, even when physical size is controlled. Women experience differences in acute intoxication (i.e., they are intoxicated at lower amounts of alcohol) and long-term consequences (e.g., women are more vulnerable to cirrhosis). Female alcohol and cocaine abusers also appear more vulnerable to developing a depressive disorder. Prescription drug use is generally more prevalent among women than men.

Barriers to Treatment for Women

There is a tremendous social stigma for substance-abusing women, particularly regarding pregnancy and motherhood. As a result, shame and guilt are exacerbated and probably discourage some women from seeking treatment. Other barriers to treatment include the following (Finkelstein, 1994):

1. Under-identification of substance abuse by professionals
2. The role of caretaker of children
3. Lack of financial as well as other resources (e.g., health insurance, safe living conditions, housing)

4. Fear of losing custody of children
5. The predominance of male-centered substance abuse treatment programs

Treatment Needs of Women

Women require the same services as men with regard to detoxification, education, support, and treatment of comorbid psychiatric conditions. However, they also require programs that provide child care services, esteem building, education of family and friends, and vocational assessment and counseling (Allen, 1995; Closser & Blow, 1993; Finkelstein, 1994).

HIV/AIDS

Prevention with Adolescents

HIV/AIDS is recognized as a major health problem in the United States. Given that AIDS is irreversible and fatal, prevention is of extreme importance (Botvin & Dusenbury, 1992). The two major mechanisms of HIV transmission are IV drug use and sexual activity, both of which are usually initiated in adolescence. Therefore, prevention activities should be directed at adolescents. For example, Botvin and Dusenbury (1992) described a prevention model to reduce the risk of HIV infection that is, essentially, an adaptation of the Life Skills Training program (described in Chapter 7). In addition to education, competence-skills training is provided to facilitate behavior change and coping.

Barriers to Treatment for Adolescents

Adolescents experience multiple barriers to health and mental health services (Berger & Levin, 1993):

1. Health services that are generally geared toward the needs of adults
2. Embarrassment about seeking care for personal health needs, especially reproductive health problems
3. Parental consent requirements
4. Concern about confidentiality
5. Transportation
6. Treatment hours conflict with school or work schedules

Barriers to Treatment and Treatment Needs of Those with HIV/AIDS

Substance abusers with HIV present multiple treatment needs. However, significant barriers exist for treatment (Berger & Levin, 1993):

1. Inability to afford treatment
2. The absence of child care services

3. Reluctance to seek medical services
4. Distrust of the medical system

In addition to these barriers to treatment, services that substance abusers with HIV receive are fragmented—substance abuse treatment programs are often not equipped to treat the significant medical problems associated with HIV. Many medical treatment programs are not equipped to treat substance abusers (Berger & Levin, 1993). It is recommended that integration of services be implemented by offering on-site care for primary medical, mental health, substance abuse, HIV/ AIDS, and formal linkages between substance abuse, psychiatric, and HIV/AIDS treatment programs.

Batki (1988) has suggested the possibility of methadone maintenance programs as central sites for treatment of opioid-abusing, HIV-positive patients. Because methadone patients maintain daily contact with the program, an intensity of contact exists that is not seen in other types of treatment. Batki (1988) proposed that methadone patients receive medical treatment, psychiatric care, and social services. However, problems with methadone programs stem from limited resources: inadequate staffing, large caseloads, and waiting lists. Also, treatment complications exist regarding problems in motivating terminally ill patients to stop drug use and concerns about terminating noncompliant patients who may deteriorate and pose greater public health risks.

THE ELDERLY POPULATION

Diagnostic Issues

Alcohol abuse among the elderly population is an underreported disorder and is a growing and serious health problem (Closser & Blow, 1993). The underreporting of alcohol use in this group reflects several factors including the use of inappropriate screening methods (developed for use with younger individuals), poor recognition of alcohol-related problems in the elderly population by patients and clinicians, and the stigma associated with identification of alcohol abuse among older persons.

Symptoms of alcohol dependence and withdrawal are more difficult to assess with older patients. Issues such as chronic illness, inadequate nutrition, and the use of medication change the sensitivity and tolerance of elderly individuals to alcohol and other substances. With the elderly population, greater sensitivity to alcohol occurs due to a decrease in the volume of total water in the body and an increase in the prevalence of chronic diseases (Closser & Blow, 1993).

Treatment of the Elderly Population

A primary concern in the treatment of older persons involves difficulties associated with withdrawal from alcohol and other substances. Withdrawal syndromes (especially alcohol) worsen with age and the severity of withdrawal episodes increases with repeated episodes (Closser & Blow, 1993). The older patient may have a greater need for more intensive treatment due to the higher prevalence of detoxification complications, medical, and psychological problems. Also, because older people are more vulnerable to cognitive impairment from substance use, treatment may be impeded. However, treatment outcomes indicate that older patients respond as well as younger patients to traditional treatment programs. Treatment is more successful for the elderly substance abuser when experienced with a homogenous peer group instead of a mixed age group (Closser & Blow, 1993). These findings should be considered when placing elderly patients in treatment groups.

THE HOMELESS POPULATION

Prevalence of Substance Abuse

Homeless people experience elevated levels of substance abuse and mental illness, compared to the general population (North & Smith, 1993a). Homeless women have lower rates of substance abuse and incarceration than homeless men; however, homeless women are more often responsible for dependent children (Smith, North, & Spitznagel, 1993). Minority groups, the unemployed, and the impoverished are overrepresented in this population.

Underutilization of Services

Despite high levels of need, there is significant underutilization of mental health services by the homeless population (North & Smith, 1993b). Underutilization appears largely due to a lack of insight or denial of need. When homeless people seek treatment they tend to overuse inpatient services, probably because waiting has caused the problem to reach undeniable crisis proportions. Therefore, increasing the access of outpatient services would be beneficial for the homeless population. Access to outpatient services can be improved by offering low-cost treatment, addressing scheduling and transportation problems, and allowing patients to see a physician or mental health care provider without a long wait. Also, intensive outreach can help improve access to outpatient services for this underserved group (North & Smith, 1993b).

REFERENCES

Allen, K. (1995). Barriers to treatment for addicted African-American women. *Journal of the National Medical Association, 87*(10), 751–756.

Arana, G. W. (1982). The impaired physician: A medical and social dilemma. *General Hospital Psychiatry, 4*, 147–154.

Batki, S. L. (1988). Treatment of intravenous drug users with AIDS: The role of methadone maintenance. *Journal of Psychoactive Drugs, 20*(2), 213–216.

Berger, J. M., & Levin, S. M. (1993). Adolescent substance abuse and HIV/AIDS: Linking the systems. *Journal of Adolescent Chemical Dependency, 2*(3–4), 49–56.

Botvin, G. J., & Dusenbury, L. (1992). Substance abuse prevention: Implications for reducing risk of HIV infection. *Psychology of Addictive Behaviors, 6*(2), 70–80.

Carlson, H. B., Dilts, S. L., & Radcliff, S. (1994). Physicians with substance abuse problems and their recovery environment: A survey. *Journal of Substance Abuse Treatment, 11*(2), 113–119.

Centrella, M. 1994. Physician addiction and impairment. Current thinking: A review. *Journal of Addictive Diseases, 13*(1), 91–105.

Closser, M. H., & Blow, F. C. (1993). Special populations: Women, ethnic minorities, and the elderly. *Recent Advances in Addictive Disorders, 16*(1), 199–209.

Finkelstein, N. (1994). Treatment issues for alcohol- and drug-dependent pregnant and parenting women. *Health & Social Work, 19*(1), 7–15.

McAuliffe, W. E., Rohman, M., Breer, P., Wyshak, G., Santangelo, S., & Magnuson, E. (1991). Alcohol use and abuse in random samples of physicians and medical students. *American Journal of Public Health, 81*(2), 177–181.

North, C. S., & Smith, E. M. (1993a). A comparison of homeless men and women: Different populations, different needs. *Community Mental Health Journal, 29*(5), 423–431.

North, C. S., & Smith, E. M. (1993b). A systematic study of mental health services utilization by homeless men and women. *Social Psychiatry and Psychiatric Epidemiology, 28*, 77–83.

Richman, J. A. (1992). Occupational stress, psychological vulnerability and alcohol-related problems over time in future physicians. *Alcoholism: Clinical and Experimental Research, 16*(2), 166–171.

Schinke, S. P., Moncher, M. S., Palleja, J., Zayas, L. H., & Schilling, R. F. (1988). Hispanic youth, substance abuse, and stress: Implications for prevention research. *The International Journal of the Addictions, 23*(8), 809–826.

Smith, E. M., North, C. S., & Spitznagel, E. L. (1993). Alcohol, drugs, and psychiatric comorbidity among homeless women: An epidemiologic study. *Journal of Clinical Psychiatry, 54*, 82–87.

Terrell, M. D. (1993). Ethnocultural factors and substance abuse: Toward culturally sensitive treatment models. *Psychology of Addictive Behaviors, 7*, 162–167.

Westermeyer, J. (1995). Cultural aspects of substance abuse and alcoholism: Assessment and management. *The Psychiatric Clinics of North America, 18*(3), 589–603.

11

LEGAL AND ETHICAL ISSUES

The following information is provided for educational purposes and is not intended to be legal advice. If a clinician encounters legal or ethical difficulties, he or she should consult with an attorney.

CONFIDENTIALITY

Rationale for Confidentiality

Confidentiality is essential to the establishment of an effective practitioner–patient relationship in the mental health field. The various organizations established to monitor and regulate counselors, psychologists, social workers, and physicians all emphasize the primary importance of this concept in their guiding principles and ethical standards (Piazza & Yeager, 1990). The intent of confidentiality is to protect the patient from any harm that might arise from the disclosure of information obtained in the practitioner–patient relationship (VandeCreek, Miars, & Herzog, 1987).

Chemical abusers often avoid treatment because of societal stigma and fears of discrimination. Consequently, federal and state laws have been enacted to protect an individual's privacy. These regulations outline the appropriate rationales for the disclosure of a patient's alcohol- or drug-related history (Lee & Bluestone, 1994). When a professional relationship is created between a patient and a counselor, psychologist, social worker, chemical dependency specialist, physician, or nurse, the practitioner must uphold certain regulatory and statutory standards (Clark & Zweben, 1989). Therefore, knowledge of those laws and guidelines relevant to substance abuse treatment and confidentiality issues, and the application by practitioners of the appropriate ethical principles to address specific dilemmas within the substance abuse field, are considered imperative (Piazza & Yeager, 1990).

Patients value confidentiality and typically prefer that little information is disclosed (VandeCreek *et al.*, 1987). Not surprisingly, within case law, the unauthorized disclosure of patient information has been identified as the primary basis for malpractice suits (discussed in Piazza & Yeager, 1990).

Federal Guidelines for Valid Consent to Disclose Information

As a result of state-to-state variation in regulations related to confidentiality, federal mandates were developed for federally funded drug and alcohol abuse programs by the Department of Health and Human Services in 1987. The federal guidelines are comprehensive and are used by nonfederally funded programs as well. According to the regulations, a valid consent form authorizing the release of patient information must include the following points (discussed in Piazza & Yeager, 1990):

1. The name or general designation of the program or person authorized to disclose the information.
2. The name or title of the individual or the name of the organization to which the information is to be disclosed.
3. The patient's name.
4. Specific purposes for which the information may be used.
5. The nature of the information to be disclosed.
6. The signature of the patient or the signature of a person authorized to give consent in the case of a minor or someone adjudicated mentally incompetent.
7. The date the consent is granted.
8. A statement that the consent may be revoked at any time (unless the disclosure has already occurred).
9. The date or conditions of expiration of consent. Consent should last no longer than reasonably necessary to serve the purpose for which it is given.

Additionally, the disclosure must be voluntarily rendered, and the clinician must also attempt to determine that the disclosure will not harm the patient or the patient's treatment. The practitioner or agency assumes full responsibility that these conditions are met prior to disclosure of patient information (Piazza & Yeager, 1990).

Disclosure without Patient Consent

There are circumstances in which mental health practitioners may disclose patient information without consent. For example, disclosure without consent is allowed in a medical emergency. Also, information may be disclosed to "qualified personnel for research, audit, or program evaluation, but the qualified personnel may not include patient-identifying information on any report or otherwise disclose patient identity" (Lee & Bluestone, 1994, p. 190).

Federal regulations also permit disclosure of patient information to qualified service organizations (QSOs) if the organization provides contractual services such as peer or professional review services, legal or accounting services, bill collection, or laboratory analysis to or for the treating agency or practitioner (Piazza & Yeager, 1990). However, this cannot occur unless a written agreement exists between the agency–practitioner and the QSO that acknowledges that the QSO is bound by the same confidentiality requirements as the provider with respect to how it receives, stores, and processes the information (Piazza & Yeager, 1990). The patient must be informed of the provider's relationship with the QSO prior to the disclosure of information and only that information necessary for the service to be performed by the QSO shall be released.

Other exceptions to confidentiality are the following (Piazza & Yeager, 1990):

1. The existence of imminent danger to self or others (the duty to protect applies)
2. Suspected child abuse
3. Competency hearings
4. Worker's compensation hearings
5. Litigation brought by the patient against the therapist
6. Court order to release information. Clinicians sometimes erroneously respond to subpoenas by disclosing requested information without patient consent. This opens clinicians to possible liability suits. Courts may issue subpoenas, either a *subpoena ad testificandum* (which orders the recipient to appear in court and answer questions), or a *subpoena duces tecum* (which orders the recipient to appear and produce all relevant files, documents, reports, papers, and notes). However, neither order compels the recipient to disclose confidential information; written consent is still required to release confidential information (Wulach, 1991). A court order issued by a judge requires that the provider disclose patient information. In this instance, a judge has determined that the information is neither privileged nor confidential (Piazza & Yeager, 1990).

Confidentiality and HIV Status

Confidentiality issues become increasingly complex and problematic when an individual's HIV-positive status is known. Such information often creates ethical and legal dilemmas for the provider who is responsible both to his or her patients and to society. In view of the severe consequences of HIV transmission, the American Psychiatric Association's (APA) code of ethics states that a physician may notify the partners of an HIV-positive patient if the disclosure is done without identifying the patient and the patient's confidentially and privacy are protected (Lee & Bluestone, 1994). It may be advisable, in order to guard against alienating the patient, to discuss the notification of partners with the patient in treatment.

Confidentiality and Illegal Behavior

Clinicians are under no obligation to report a patient's past or current illegal behavior (Piazza & Yeager, 1990).

Confidentiality and Minors

The adolescent suffering from a psychoactive substance use disorder is considered a minor and consequently, in some states, may not be asked to provide an informed consent for treatment (Dyer & MacIntyre, 1992). Parents are typically required to give their consent for the treatment of any child. However, in some states, such as New Jersey, the law authorizes minors to obtain treatment for substance abuse without a parent or guardian's consent (Wulach, 1991). A minor, 14 years or older, may also request hospital admission for psychiatric treatment without a parent's or guardian's consent. In New Jersey, treating physicians (and probably all mental health professionals) are permitted, but not obligated, by law to inform a minor's parents or guardians about any treatment provided, without the minor's consent (Wulach, 1991).

RESPONSIBILITY TO DIAGNOSE AND TREAT SUBSTANCE USE DISORDERS

An ethical responsibility exists for the practitioner to identify and appropriately treat (or refer) a patient's psychoactive substance use disorder. Practitioners and researchers agree about the benefits of early identification of a psychoactive substance use disorder. A missed diagnosis or misdiagnosis of a substance use disorder may lead to treatment errors and devastating consequences for the patient (Lee & Bluestone, 1994). Clark and Zweben (1989) reported that incorrect treatment, failure to diagnose, and incorrect diagnosis can result in malpractice claims against psychologists. For all psychotherapists, malpractice suits are more frequent in cases involving issues of chemical dependence than in other areas of mental health treatment (Clark & Zweben, 1989).

Given the diversity of professional disciplines and approaches to treatment, a standard of care for substance abuse is difficult to articulate (Clark & Zweben, 1989). A standard of care refers to those actions expected by similarly trained practitioners presented with similar factual situations (Clark & Zweben, 1989). A legal and ethical duty exists to refer a patient if the practitioner discovers, or with reasonable diligence should have discovered, that the patient requires a form of specialized care not offered by the provider (Clark & Zweben, 1989). This mandate is extremely critical in the treatment of the dually diagnosed patient. Although a practitioner may focus on a circumscribed area of treatment (e.g., detoxification) of an individual with a psychoactive substance abuse disorder, he or she maintains a professional responsibility to recognize any other problem that the patient may be experiencing and to refer the patient for appropriate treatment (Clark & Zweben, 1989).

COERCED TREATMENT

Driving While Intoxicated (DWI) Programs

Treatment programs designed to provide services to individuals convicted of driving while intoxicated (DWI) present ethical dilemmas to providers. Typically, patients court-ordered to attend DWI programs must comply with treatment recommendations in order to maintain or regain their driving privileges. The use of treatment modalities, such as inpatient detoxification and rehabilitation or Antabuse treatment to help patients attain sobriety, may raise ethical questions about whether patient compliance is freely given or coerced (Lee & Bluestone, 1994). To assess these issues, both the patient's needs and society's interest in safeguarding the public must be weighed. Especially in those cases in which an individual presents with a history of psychoactive substance abuse that is not clear cut, the practitioner must guard against the consequences of an erroneous treatment decision or recommendation for the patient, the patient's family, and society. The prudent course is to obtain a second opinion in order to achieve a positive treatment outcome (Lee & Bluestone, 1994).

Referral for Treatment by Social Service Agencies

Individuals who attend methadone treatment programs are frequently referred by social service agencies (Lee & Bluestone, 1994). These agencies often have dual agendas: to refer patients for needed substance abuse services and to ensure that public money is not used to support substance abuse. The motivation for patients to become involved in methadone treatment and other programs for chemical abuse in order to qualify for or maintain their public assistance funding is probably not uncommon. Mental health professionals are ethically bound to present to social agencies an accurate representation of a patient's participation in treatment. Correspondence should clearly and accurately reflect the patient's level of participation; a generic letter does not comply with such standards (Lee & Bluestone, 1994).

Treatment of Pregnant Mothers

Abuse of various substances, including alcohol, is associated with a range of impairments in newborns, including (a) low birth weight, (b) decreased head circumference, (c) irritability, (d) sudden infant death syndrome (SIDS), (e) neurobehavioral dysfunction, and (f) intellectual impairment (Hawk, 1994). The fetal damage may be due to the direct effects of drugs or associated behaviors such as the poor quality of prenatal care, maternal health, or nutrition (Hawk, 1994). Concern about the potential harm to newborns has led to societal endorsement of legal interventions to prevent substance abuse by pregnant women. However, legal actions against substance-abusing pregnant women conflict with the constitutional rights of privacy, bodily integrity, and liberty (Andrews & Patterson, 1995). The balance of constitutional rights and societal interest in protection of the fetus remains precarious. State and local authorities have utilized a variety of legal actions in an effort to detect cases of maternal substance abuse. These actions include the mandatory reporting of drug-exposed newborns to child welfare agencies, involuntary drug testing of pregnant women and newborns, mandatory reporting of positive drug test results to law enforcement agencies, involuntary commitment to substance abuse treatment facilities, and criminal prosecution or incarceration (Andrews & Patterson, 1995; Finkelstein, 1994).

Substance-abusing pregnant women have been prosecuted on such charges as child abuse or neglect, child endangerment, drug possession, contributing to the delinquency of a minor, and delivering a controlled dangerous substance to a minor (Hawk, 1994). These legal actions have created a debate regarding their usefulness; these interventions have created barriers for women seeking drug abuse services or prenatal care (Andrews & Patterson, 1995; Finkelstein, 1994; Hawk, 1994). Interventions to assess substance abuse during pregnancy and to mandate treatment have been characterized as coercive or unethical (Andrews & Patterson, 1995; Finkelstein, 1994; Hawk, 1994). Additional problems face incarcerated pregnant women who often receive little or no substance abuse treatment, prenatal care, or nutritional counseling (Andrews & Patterson, 1995; Finkelstein, 1994).

It is recommended that rather than criminalize pregnant mothers, more accessible and effective treatment should be offered. Barriers for those women seeking treatment include the following (Andrews & Patterson, 1995):

1. Fear of prosecution
2. Separation from children
3. Reliance on male-centered models of treatment
4. Inability to pay for services
5. Inadequate obstetrical services

Programs should offer financial assistance, infant and child care, detoxification, and obstetrical services to female drug offenders (Hawk, 1994).

AMERICANS WITH DISABILITIES ACT (ADA)

Description of the ADA

The Americans with Disabilities Act (ADA) was passed in 1990 (Shaw, MacGillis, & Dvorchik, 1994). It is, essentially, a civil rights law established to protect Americans with disabilities from employment discrimination (Jones, 1994; Shaw *et al.*, 1994). Implications of this law are relevant to individuals with substance use disorders. An individual with a disability is defined as "an individual with: (a) a physical or mental impairment that substantially limits one or more of the major life activities of such individual; (b) a record of such impairment; or (c) being regarded as having such an impairment" (in Jones, 1994, p. 155).

Application of the ADA to Substance Abusers

Interestingly, users of illegal substances and alcohol users are categorized separately and receive differential protection under the ADA (Jones, 1994; Shaw *et al.*, 1994). Someone engaged in the current use of illegal drugs is open to disciplinary action (i.e., is not protected); but someone currently using alcohol is protected under the ADA. The differential protection stems from the view of alcohol abuse as a disability; the current use of illegal substances is not considered a disability. However, a person who has used illegal substances in the past is considered disabled if he or she no longer engages in illegal drug use and has successfully completed (or is in the process of completing) a substance abuse treatment program or is otherwise rehabilitated. Use of an illegal substance is defined in terms of the nonmedically supervised use of any Schedule I-V drugs (see Chapter 1 for discussion of the federal classification system for drugs).

An employer can insist on, and enforce, the maintenance of a drug-free environment (in accordance with the Drug Free Workplace Act of 1988) as long as it is applied equally to all employees. The employer may also test prospective or current employees for alcohol or drug use and still comply with the provisions of the ADA (Shaw *et al.*, 1994). If an employee violates the alcohol/drug policy on the job, he or she is open to disciplinary action. However, according to the ADA, if work impairment related to alcohol abuse is observed, an employer is obligated to make reasonable accommodations to assist that person (e.g., offer employee assistance program [EAP] services, leave of absence, flexible work schedule to accommodate treatment, job restructuring, or AA meetings on the premises). If work-related performance problems are observed in response to the use of illegal substances, there is no ADA requirement for the employer to make accommodations.

To summarize and clarify the application of the ADA to substance abusers:

1. Anyone found using drugs or alcohol on the job is open to disciplinary action due to violation of the Drug Free Workplace Act of 1988.
2. Work-related impairment due to substance use/abuse:
   a. Alcohol (current or past use) is protected by the ADA and reasonable accomodations must be made to assist this individual.
   b. Illegal drug use (current) is not protected by the ADA and the employer is not obligated to make accommodations.
   c. Illegal drug use (past) is protected by the ADA and reasonable accommodations must be made to assist this individual.

Some concerns relate to the ambiguous time frame of the "current user of illegal drugs" status (Jones, 1994). At what point does someone become a former user of drugs? Also, the point has been made that the law may have a regressive effect for substance abusers. Current users of illegal drugs may not seek treatment for fear of jeopardizing their jobs and receiving no protection under the law (Jones, 1994).

REFERENCES

Andrews, B. A., & Patterson, E. G. (1995). Searching for solutions to alcohol and other drug abuse during pregnancy: Ethics, values, and constitutional principles. *Social Work, 40*, 55–64.

Clark, H. W., & Zweben, J. E. (1989). Legal vulnerabilities in the treatment of chemically dependent dual diagnosis patients. *Journal of Psychoactive Drugs, 21*(2), 251–257.

Dyer, A. R., & MacIntyre, J. C. (1992). Utilization of private child and adolescent services: Ethical considerations. *Administration and Policy in Mental Health, 19*, 139–149.

Finkelstein, N. (1994). Treatment issues for alcohol- and drug-dependent pregnant and parenting women. *Health and Social Work, 19*, 7–15.

Hawk, M. A. (1994). How social policies make matters worse: The case of maternal substance abuse. *The Journal of Drug Issues, 24*(3), 517–526.

Jones, N. (1994). The alcohol and drug provisions of the ADA: Implications for employers and employees. In S. M. Bruyere & J. O'Keeffe (Eds.), *Implications of the Americans with Disabilities Act for psychology* (pp. 151–168). Washington, DC: American Psychological Association.

Lee, H. K., & Bluestone, H. (1994). Ethical and forensic considerations in substance abuse treatment. In H. Bluestone, S. Travin, & S. B. Marlowe (Eds.), *Psychiatric-legal decision making by the mental health practitioner: The clinician as de facto magistrate* (pp. 187–201). New York: John Wiley & Sons.

Piazza, N. J., & Yeager, R. D. (1990). Federal confidentiality regulations for substance abuse treatment facilities: A case in applied ethics. *Journal of Mental Health Counseling, 12*, 120–128.

Shaw, L. R., MacGillis, P. W., & Dvorchik, K. M.(1994). Alcoholism and the Americans with Disabilities Act: Obligations and accommodations. *Rehabilitation Counseling Bulletin, 38*(2), 108–123.

VandeCreek, L., Miars, R. D., & Herzog, C. E. (1987). Client anticipations and preferences for confidentiality of records. *Journal of Counseling Psychology, 34*, 62–67.

Wulach, J. S. (1991). *Law & mental health professionals: New Jersey.* Washington, DC: American Psychological Association.

EPILOGUE

The abuse of psychoactive substances is a major problem in the United States. Due to the prevalence of alcohol and drug abuse, clinicians frequently encounter these problems in practice. Substance abuse disorders are complex and multifaceted. Fortunately, there is a surfeit of information on these disorders. The existence of a large database is advantageous for clinicians. However, a challenge exists to acquire and assimilate the information, and to apply it effectively in clinical settings. We set out to faithfully present the current thinking, as reflected in professional journals and books, on important aspects of psychoactive substance use disorders. Whether the reader's motivation for obtaining this publication was for education, research, or preparation for a professional certification examination (or some combination of these motives), we hope that we have assisted you to achieve your goal(s).

Involvement in professional associations can assist individuals who desire to enhance their knowledge and skills, and to interact with other clinicians working with substance abusers. For mental health professionals, state and national associations exist for most discplines. Interested readers are encouraged to contact their respective associations.

INDEX